Wild, Bold, and Ambitious

Unleash Your Inner Entrepreneur

By: Sheriff Thaver

Contents

Dedications.. i

Acknowledgments.. ii

About the Author... iv

Author's Note.. v

Preface.. vi

Introduction... vii

Part 1 - Traits of Entrepreneurs 1

Introduction: The DNA of a Successful Entrepreneur 2

Section 1.1: Foundational Traits for Entrepreneurial Success 3

1.1.1.Visionary Thinking.. 5

1.1.2.Emotional Intelligence 9

1.1.3.Passion and Intrinsic Drive 13

1.1.4.Confidence and Self-Belief.. 17

1.1.5.Grit - Resilience, Perseverance, and Discipline 21

Section 1.2: Traits for Navigating Challenges and Opportunities................. 25

1.2.1. Adaptability and Flexibility.. 28

1.2.2. Risk-Taking.. 32

1.2.3. Creativity and Innovation... 37

1.2.4. Resourcefulness.. 42

1.2.5. Ability to Take Initiative.. 47

Section 1.3: Traits for Building & Sustaining a Thriving Business 51

1.3.1. Strong Work Ethic 54

1.3.2. Networking and Relationship-Building 58

1.3.3. Customer-Centric Mindset 62

1.3.4. Financial Acumen.. 66

1.3.5. Long-Term Perspective 70

Part 2 - Entrepreneur's Journey.. 74

Introduction: A Crash Course in Conquering the Business World 75

Section 2.1: Realizing the Dream.. 77

2.1.1. Where Dreams Begin - Ideation.. 77

2.1.2. Where Passion Meets Purpose - Planning............................... 82

2.1.3. Show Me the Money! - Securing Financing 87

2.1.4. Where Vision Takes Shape - Business Set-Up 91

2.1.5. Showtime - Launch 96

Section 2.2: Where the Magic Happens - Operations 100

2.2.1. Running a Business - Like a Pro 103

2.2.2. Keeping Your Business in the Black (and Your Sanity Intact)......... 107

2.2.3. Building Your Dream Team... 111

2.2.4. Light the Path to Your Brilliance! - Marketing 116

2.2.6. Keeping the Love Alive! - Customers Service.......................... 125

Section 2.3: Evolving and Closing the Journey 129

2.3.1. Getting It Done and Making It Count - Deliverables.................. 129

2.3.2. Doing Well by Doing Good - Social Responsibility 134

2.3.3. Bring in the Big Guns - Investor Timing................................ 139

2.3.4. The Grand Finale - Exit.. 145

Part 3 - Entrepreneur's Tools... 150

Introduction to Part 3: Entrepreneur's Tools 151

Section 3.1: Foundational Frameworks 152

3.1.1. The "GUIDE" Blueprint: Craft Your Business's True North 152

3.1.2. FRAME Blueprint: Building a Business Model That Works 154

Section 3.2: Financial and Operational Tools 156

3.2.1. The "PROFIT" Model - Master Your Finances 156

3.2.2. "FLOWS": Your Cash Flow Compass for Driving Growth 158

Section 3.3: Execution and Growth Tools 160

3.3.1. The "PRODUCTIVE" Model: Managing Your Time Better 160

3.3.2. The "CREATE" Model: Building a Sales Funnel 165

Bonus Content 167

Business Plan Framework 167

Investor Pitch Playbook: Nailing Your First Impression 175

Startup Failures: Key Insights and Lessons Learned 182

Disclaimer 188

Dedications

This book is a compass, a companion, and your call to rise for every courageous founder, dreamer, and risk-taker who has ever felt stuck, uncertain, or overwhelmed. Your fortitude and determination have significantly influenced this journey. I hope it will guide and inspire as we collaborate to empower 10,000 entrepreneurs by 2029.

Acknowledgments

Writing *Wild, Bold, and Ambitious* has been an exhilarating and transformative journey, and it would not have been possible without the incredible people who supported, inspired, and guided me along the way.

First and foremost, I want to extend my heartfelt gratitude to **Shak**, my co-writer, whose contributions were invaluable in bringing this book to life, with over three decades of international business expertise and a proven track record of driving success across continents. Shak played a pivotal role in business turnarounds, high-stakes negotiations, mergers & acquisitions, joint ventures, and strategic alliances. With his hands-on experience, Shak continues to empower businesses with innovative strategies and a forward-thinking approach to sustainable growth.

To my wife, **Perviz**, your encouragement and patience have been my anchor. You've shown me the power of belief, reminding me to stay true to my vision even during moments of doubt. Thank you for being my biggest cheerleader, a constant source of strength and light guiding me through this incredible endeavour.

I sincerely thank my clients, colleagues, friends and associates who have generously provided thoughtful feedback and honest perspectives. Your willingness to engage with early drafts, ask challenging questions, and offer constructive advice has enriched this book immeasurably. Your insights have helped me refine its content and ensure it delivers meaningful value to entrepreneurs everywhere.

I also acknowledge AI's assistance in processing, wordsmithing, and editing content, which helped refine this book. This tool provided invaluable support during the creative process.

Thank you to the countless entrepreneurs and dreamers who inspired this book through your stories, struggles, and successes. This book reflects the lessons we've learned together, the shared challenges we've overcome, and the boundless passion that drives us all to reach for more.

Finally, thank you, the reader, for allowing me to be part of your entrepreneurial journey. This book is for you, and I hope it serves as a source of inspiration, guidance, and empowerment as you navigate your path toward Wild, Bold, and Ambitious success.

Sheriff Thaver

About the Author

Sheriff Thaver is a seasoned entrepreneur, strategic business coach, and consultant with over two decades of experience helping businesses and individuals unlock their potential and achieve lasting success. As a trusted strategic thought partner, Sheriff has guided over a hundred entrepreneurs through the complexities of building and scaling businesses, offering clarity, confidence, and actionable insights. With an MBA from the Sobey School of Business, he has been involved in seven startups, collaborated with global organizations, consulted for the Government of Canada, and empowered hundreds of enterprising people to realize their visions. His passion, expertise, and practical wisdom infuse every page of this book, making it an essential companion for new entrepreneurs.

Ready to take the leap?

Get started today and transform your dreams into reality.

www.wildboldandambitious.com

Author's Note

As you turn these pages, know that you're tapping into the insights of someone who has walked your path. I didn't want to write a textbook or a feel-good storybook. I wanted to create something tangible - a lifeline for entrepreneurs. It's a **practical playbook for the wild, bold, and ambitious**, a tool-packed guide I wish someone had given me when I felt stuck, when cash was tight, and when self-doubt was creeping in.

The case studies in this book are adapted or fictionalized, but their lessons are raw, authentic, and deeply relevant to your journey. Each example is here to remind you that you are not alone, that the struggles you face are shared by many, and that there's a way forward - always.

Now is your time. As you dive into these pages, I encourage you to see yourself in these stories, draw strength from the lessons, and dream bigger than ever. The tools and strategies in this book should inspire you to take bold action, believe in your vision, and push through every obstacle with resilience and determination.

Entrepreneurship is not for the faint of heart, but you're here because you're ready to make a difference, not just for yourself, but for your team, customers, and the world.

Remember, every great entrepreneur started where you are now - with an idea, a dream, and the courage to take the first step. Let this book be your companion as you build the life and business you've always imagined. Together, let's make it happen.

Thank you for trusting me to be part of your journey. Your success is within reach, and I can't wait to see the incredible things you'll achieve.

Preface

Welcome to Wild, Bold, and Ambitious, book one in the "Built to Strive" series. Writing this practical playbook has been a profoundly personal journey rooted in two decades of experience as an entrepreneur, strategic business coach, and consultant.

My work has always been about empowering individuals such as yourself to create something amazing. For me, it is not merely a business but a purposeful life with courage, clarity, and conviction. This book is my attempt to share what I have learned through thousands of hours working with entrepreneurs, navigating uncertainty, and celebrating wins.

Entrepreneurship is not a straight line; it's more like navigating through unpredictable waters. There are high tides, storms that come out of nowhere, periods of calm, and the thrill of discovering new shores. You become who you never knew you could be along the way. You become stronger, wiser, and more grounded in who you are and what you stand for.

But let me be clear: this book doesn't promise shortcuts or quick fixes. Building something that lasts takes resilience, focus, and a willingness to view mistakes as learning opportunities to improve and grow. It offers a compass: a practical, principle-driven guide to help you navigate the highs and lows with purpose.

My mission is to **empower 10,000 entrepreneurs by 2029**, equipping them with the tools, mindset, and support they need to build purpose-driven, thriving businesses. If this book helps you take even one bold step forward, then we're one step closer to that goal.

If you're holding this book, chances are you already feel the spark of something bigger. I hope this becomes a companion on your path, not just to business success but to becoming an entrepreneur who leads with compassion and builds their vision with a deep sense of purpose, courage, and integrity.

Here's to your journey,

Sheriff Thaver

Introduction

This book is for bold thinkers and big dreamers who want to build more than a business. It's about creating a legacy.

Why Does This Book Matter?

Entrepreneurship is as much a journey of self-discovery as it is about building a business. It's where vision meets action, passion meets perseverance, and ambition meets strategy. Success doesn't happen by chance - it happens by design. That's where *Wild, Bold, and Ambitious* steps in.

This book will help you navigate every stage of your journey - from brainstorming bold ideas to executing them precisely and purposefully.

The names of individuals, businesses, products, services, examples, and results featured in case studies have been modified or fictionalized.

What to Expect in This Book?

1. The Traits of a Wild, Bold, and Ambitious Entrepreneur (*Part 1*)

Dive into the DNA of a successful entrepreneur. This part will explore the traits that successful entrepreneurs possess and how these traits can be developed and refined. Some of these traits include visionary thinking, emotional intelligence, adaptability, and creativity. You will learn how to develop these characteristics to thrive in the face of challenges and embrace new opportunities.

2. The Entrepreneur's Journey (*Part 2*)

Every business begins with a dream. But turning that dream into reality requires more than enthusiasm; it requires strategy, execution, and grit. This part guides you through the entrepreneurial lifecycle, from ideation and planning to launching your business, scaling operations, building a team, navigating growth, and finally, evolving and exiting your business while leaving a lasting impact.

3. Tools for the Ambitious Entrepreneur (*Part 3*)

Great entrepreneurs know that tools can transform ambition into achievement. This part equips you with essential models, templates, and strategies to tackle the complexities of entrepreneurship. You'll gain practical resources to operate efficiently and confidently, from financial planning and time management to building a sales funnel and crafting investor pitches (In the bonus section).

What will you gain from this book?

- **How to Think Like an Entrepreneur:** Cultivate a mindset that embraces risk, fosters innovation, and turns obstacles into opportunities.
- **How to Build a Thriving Business:** Learn how to master the fundamentals of planning, execution, and scaling with actionable strategies.
- **How to Sustain and Grow:** Develop systems, processes, and tools that ensure long-term success in a fast-changing world.

Embrace the Wild Ride

The entrepreneurial path is challenging, inspiring, and pushes you to grow. *Wild, Bold, and Ambitious* is your companion on this thrilling journey, providing you with the insights, frameworks, and motivation to succeed on your terms.

Let's dive in and unleash the Wild, Bold, and Ambitious Entrepreneur within you. The adventure starts now!

Part 1 - Traits of Entrepreneurs

Introduction: The DNA of a Successful Entrepreneur

What sets entrepreneurs apart from the rest of the crowd? It's not just having a killer idea or being in the right place at the right time (although that certainly helps). The secret sauce lies in the unique traits that drive entrepreneurs to turn their visions into reality, survive the rollercoaster of challenges, and thrive in a world where most would throw in the towel. Part 1 goes in-depth into the traits that make up the entrepreneurial spirit - the same traits that drive success, even in the face of adversity. The traits are grouped into three sections, each representing a pivotal phase in the journey of an entrepreneur:

Section 1.1: Foundational Traits for Entrepreneurial Success

This section explores the inherent characteristics that form the foundation for entrepreneurial endeavours. Visionary thinking, passion, and resilience help entrepreneurs like you build a strong foundation for their entrepreneurial journey.

Section 1.2: Traits for Navigating Challenges and Opportunities

Adaptability, creativity, and risk-taking become essential once challenges arise and opportunities present themselves. This section identifies the traits that enable entrepreneurs to succeed in an ever-changing business environment.

Section 1.3: Traits for Creating and Sustaining a Successful Business

Creating and maintaining a successful business requires consistent effort and strategic thinking. This section examines traits like financial acumen, a customer-centric mindset, and networking ability that enable entrepreneurs to create sustainable growth.

These traits aren't just checkboxes - they're the foundation of entrepreneurship. And as we delve into each one, you'll understand how they come together to create the pillars of successful entrepreneurs and how you can develop them to unleash your potential. Whether you're just starting or a seasoned entrepreneur, understanding and embracing these traits is key to turning your dreams into reality.

Section 1.1: Foundational Traits for Entrepreneurial Success

Case Study: Built to Succeed

The Five Foundational Traits Every Entrepreneur Needs

Sam and Tham were childhood friends who shared equal love and passion for technology. They both dreamed of launching their own company one day. As they grew up, they went their separate ways to create something innovative and revolutionary that excited them.

Sam had a clear vision of what he wanted to do. He had long thought about a future where smart home devices would integrate with each other, making life simpler for their users. He spent weeks studying market trends, identifying gaps, and brainstorming ideas. He wanted to create a platform where all these devices could connect together.

At the same time, Tham was just as enthusiastic about being an entrepreneur but lacked focus. His ideas were all over the place, from AI-enhanced pet toys to blockchain technology for supply chains. He pursued whatever seemed trendy, hoping something would stick.

Driven by his vision, Sam poured himself into his work. He was passionate, working late nights coding prototypes and networking with investors and potential collaborators during the day. His enthusiasm was infectious; he spoke about his idea with so much passion that people were drawn to him. Tham, however, had difficulty maintaining his enthusiasm. While he started strong, he tended to lose steam when the initial excitement faded or when challenges arose. He jumped from one project to the next without a deep connection to any concept.

Both Sam and Tham faced obstacles, as all entrepreneurs do. Sam's first major obstacle was during a live investor demo. His prototype crashed dramatically in front of a room full of potential investors. The embarrassment was overwhelming, but Sam did not let it define him. After the demo, he stayed up all night analyzing what went wrong. By morning, he had a solution: his technical expertise and resilience when under pressure impressed the investors. Tham faced criticism, too, primarily for not having a clear business model. Rather than working on the feedback, he allowed it to discourage him. "Perhaps this just isn't for me," he said, shelving yet another incomplete project.

Sam's confidence was instrumental in his success. Even when he didn't know everything, he believed in his vision and his ability to bring it to life. This conviction instilled faith, not only from investors but also from the small team he had assembled. They worked tirelessly, feeding off his energy and self-assurance. Tham, however, struggled with self-doubt. He hesitated in meetings, second-guessed his decisions, and often deferred to others. He struggled to rally support or take bold steps without confidence.

While Sam's platform began to take shape, he remained disciplined. He prioritised milestones, avoided distractions, and focused solely on delivering a product that addressed tangible problems. Tham, in contrast, often got sidetracked by new ideas.

Two years later, their outcomes couldn't have been more different. Sam's smart home platform launched to rave reviews. Users loved its ease of use, and investors clamoured to finance the next growth phase. His firm, once merely an aspiration, was now expanding internationally. On the other hand, Tham was still pursuing "the next big thing," jumping from idea to idea without ever following through.

Their story is a powerful reminder of what it takes to succeed as an entrepreneur. Sam's journey highlights the importance of having a well-defined vision, relentless passion, the resilience to overcome setbacks, the confidence to inspire others, and the self-discipline to remain focused. Yet, Tham's experience puts into perspective what occurs when such qualities are lacking. Their struggles give us a real picture of the entrepreneurial experience through its highs and lows and the traits that make the difference between success and stagnation.

1.1.1. Visionary Thinking

The Power of visionary thinking, "Thinking Beyond Today," makes great entrepreneurs stand out. It's about looking past what we see right now and imagining new possibilities for the future. Instead of just dreaming big, it's about making a real plan to turn those dreams into reality.

Leaders like Steve Jobs didn't settle for small changes; they aimed for big, groundbreaking shifts that changed entire industries. These visionary leaders don't wait for trends to occur; they predict them and shape their businesses to lead the change.

But having a vision isn't enough - you need to take action. A good vision inspires people, brings teams together, and creates a shared sense of purpose that keeps everyone motivated, even in challenging times. It encourages bold thinking and helps find innovative solutions that might otherwise be overlooked.

Focusing only on short-term goals can cause businesses to stagnate. Without a long-term vision, companies often react to situations instead of being proactive, struggling to stay ahead in an ever-changing landscape. Visionary entrepreneurs avoid this trap by thinking strategically, embracing innovation, and staying open to new possibilities.

This segment will guide you in developing a visionary mindset that turns ideas into action, fuels long-term success, and positions your company as a leader instead of a follower.

Let's explore how Sam and Tham succeeded (or not) in visionary thinking and the lessons we can learn from their journey.

Step with Key Focuses	Sam and Tham's Implementation Journey
Define Your Purpose and Mission - Anchor your vision with meaningful goals.	Sam spent weeks reflecting on his motivations, writing a mission statement to transform smart homes.

- Create a long-term mission statement. - Focus on purpose over fleeting trends.	Tham skipped this step, chasing trends without grounding them in a clear purpose.
Engage in Future-Oriented Thinking - Visualize your business's long-term trajectory. - Identify your role in the larger ecosystem. - Plan for sustainability and impact.	Sam used mind maps to outline long-term goals, envisioning the future of his company. Tham focused on short-term ideas, ignoring broader impacts.
Stay Informed and Curious - Cultivate curiosity about industry trends. - Draw inspiration from diverse fields. - Stay aware of external market influences.	Sam regularly read industry reports, attended conferences, and sought inspiration from other fields. Tham stuck to tech buzzwords and missed broader opportunities.
Surround Yourself with Visionaries - Build a network of inspiring, innovative individuals. - Seek fresh perspectives to challenge your thinking. - Engage in collaborative growth.	Sam attended networking events and mastermind sessions to connect with innovative thinkers. Tham avoided going to events and networking, sticking to his comfort zone.
Break Down Vision into Milestones - Segment your vision into	Sam used project management tools to divide his vision into clear, actionable steps.

actionable steps. - Use tools to track and manage progress. - Ensure steady movement toward your ultimate goals.	Tham lacked structure, frequently losing focus.
Communicate Your Vision Clearly - Create pitches that resonate with stakeholders. - Align team members with your vision. - Use clear communication to build enthusiasm.	Sam crafted compelling pitches that inspired investors and team members. Tham struggled to articulate his ideas, failing to gain buy-in.
Continuously Adjust Your Vision - Regularly review and refine your progress. - Adapt plans based on feedback and trends. - Keep your Vision relevant and flexible.	Sam held quarterly reviews to track progress, gather feedback, and adjust plans. Tham focussed on day-to-day tasks and lost track of his goals over time.

Key Takeaways:

- Adopt a forward-thinking mindset and specific habits, and take deliberate action.
- Define a bold vision, break it into clear milestones, and build a network that supports your growth.
- Visionary thinking drives results. Turn big ideas into real achievements with focus and strategy.

Self-Assessment: Are You Thinking Like a Visionary?

Rate yourself on each statement from 1 (Never) to 5 (Always):

1. I have a clear mission and purpose that drives my work.
2. I spend time envisioning the long-term impact of my ideas and business.
3. I stay informed about trends and changes that may shape the future.
4. I seek inspiration from people, industries, and ideas outside my immediate field.
5. I imagine bold possibilities and future scenarios that go beyond current limitations.
6. I break down my vision into actionable milestones to make progress.
7. I communicate my vision clearly to my team and stakeholders.
8. I revisit and refine my vision regularly based on new insights and changes.

Score Interpretation:

- **35-40**: Strong visionary. Clear, ambitious, and inspiring. You can drive long-term growth.
- **25-34**: Moderately effective. Sharpen focus and alignment to enhance impact.
- **15-24**: Needs work. Build purpose, future-thinking, and strategic clarity.
- **Below 15**: At risk. Develop a clear and compelling vision urgently.

Author's Tip: Set aside time to imagine your industry's future and your business's role in shaping it. Share this vision to inspire your team, drive innovation, and create lasting impact.

1.1.2. Emotional Intelligence

The Power of Emotional Intelligence, "Leading with Empathy," separates successful entrepreneurs from those who struggle to connect, collaborate, and lead effectively. It's the ability to understand your emotions, empathize with others, and manage relationships that foster trust, teamwork, and resilience. Emotional intelligence isn't just about being nice; it's about cultivating self-awareness and emotional mastery to drive better decision-making, build strong teams, and navigate entrepreneurship's emotional highs and lows.

Entrepreneurs like Oprah Winfrey harnessed emotional intelligence to create deep connections with their audiences and teams, building trust and loyalty that propelled their brands to global success. Emotionally intelligent leaders build environments where individuals feel valued, heard, and inspired - enhancing morale, teamwork, and productivity.

Emotional intelligence, however, needs to be practiced deliberately to build. Without it, entrepreneurs may become reactive, disconnected, and isolated from their teams and customers. Ineffective emotional management usually leads to impulsive choices, broken relationships, and lost opportunities for growth and innovation.

This segment will guide you in developing emotional intelligence skills that strengthen your leadership, improve your relationships, and propel sustainable business success.

Let's see how Sam and Tham - a story of two contrasting entrepreneurs - exemplified (or did not demonstrate) emotional intelligence and what we can learn from their experience.

Step with Key Focuses	Sam and Tham's Implementation Journey
Develop Self-Awareness - Know your feelings and how they influence your behaviour.	Sam kept a daily journal to reflect on his emotions and how they influenced his decisions.

- Identify triggers and emotional patterns. - Reflect on personal strengths and areas for growth.	Tham seldom examined his feelings and tended to be impulsive, not considering how his emotions impacted his leadership.
Practice Self-Regulation - Regulate emotional responses, particularly in times of stress. - Remain calm and level-headed during trying times.	Sam took time before responding to tense situations, breathing deeply to remain calm. Tham easily lost his temper when under stress, causing tension and confusion in his team.
Develop Empathy - Actively listen to hear other people's points of view. - Demonstrate care and concern for your customers and team. - Acknowledge other people's feelings and experiences.	Sam listened to the concerns of his employees and sympathized with their problems. Tham ignored team feedback, acting indifferent and aloof.
Build Strong Relationships - Encourage trust by practicing open communication. - Demonstrate appreciation and recognition. - Take time to foster professional relationships.	Sam regularly acknowledged his team members' efforts and fostered a supportive workplace culture. Tham seldom provided recognition, causing disengagement and high turnover.
Enhance Social Skills - Communicate openly and confidently. - Manage conflict constructively. - Encourage collaboration and teamwork.	Sam promoted open discussions to address conflicts and encourage cooperation. Tham avoided confrontation, allowing issues to boil and damage team morale.

Demonstrate Motivation and Optimism - Maintain a positive outlook, even during setbacks. - Lead your team with passion and purpose. - Stay committed to long-term vision.	Sam remained optimistic during tough times, inspiring his team to stay focused and persistent. Tham became discouraged easily, spreading negativity and doubt.
Practice Emotional Resilience - Bounce back from setbacks and failures. - Maintain emotional equilibrium during adversity. - Learn from challenging experiences to become stronger.	Sam considered setbacks as chances to learn to remain emotionally balanced through adversity. Tham struggled to recover from setbacks, often feeling defeated and stuck.

Key Takeaways:

- To build trust and strong connections, lead with self-awareness, empathy, and emotional control.
- Practice emotional resilience, stay optimistic, and foster teamwork for lasting success.
- Use emotional intelligence to create loyal teams, deepen customer relationships, and lead authentically.

Self-Assessment: Are You Leading with Emotional Intelligence?

Rate yourself on each statement from 1 (Never) to 5 (Always):

1. I regularly reflect on my emotions and how they impact my decisions.
2. I stay calm and manage my reactions under stress or pressure.
3. I actively listen to understand others' perspectives and emotions.
4. I express empathy and show concern for my team and customers.
5. I foster trust through open communication and appreciation.
6. I address conflicts constructively and promote collaboration.
7. I stay optimistic and inspire my team, even during setbacks.
8. I demonstrate emotional resilience and bounce back from failures.

Score Interpretation:

- **35-40:** Strong emotional intelligence - you lead with empathy, self-awareness, and resilience.
- **25-34:** Moderate emotional intelligence - targeted growth can boost leadership and relationships.
- **15-24:** Developing emotional intelligence - focus on self-awareness, empathy, and regulation.
- **Below 15:** Build your EQ to improve trust and leadership impact.

Author's Tip: Schedule regular reflection sessions to understand your emotional responses in different situations. Practice empathy in every conversation - genuinely listening can open doors to trust, innovation, and meaningful leadership.

1.1.3. Passion and Intrinsic Drive

Passion and intrinsic drive are the unstoppable forces that keep entrepreneurs moving forward, even when the odds are stacked against them. They are the internal engines that push you to wake up early, work late, and remain committed to your mission long after the initial excitement fades. True passion is about a deep, personal connection to your work that sustains you through setbacks and challenges.

Entrepreneurs like Sara Blakely didn't rely solely on external motivation or validation. Their unrelenting passion and intrinsic drive powered them to push boundaries, take risks, and innovate in ways others wouldn't dare. They didn't just start companies; they pursued missions they believed in wholeheartedly.

But passion alone isn't enough if it's not coupled with focused action. Intrinsic drive transforms passion into a relentless pursuit. It keeps you disciplined when things are difficult, sparks innovative solutions when obstacles appear, and helps you to keep moving, even as progress is slow.

When entrepreneurs lack intrinsic drive, they tend to be inconsistent. They may be enthusiastic about projects initially, but lose momentum easily when challenged.

This segment will guide you to understand and develop passion and intrinsic drive - the forces that sustain your energy, sharpen your attention and ignite long-term success.

Let's see how Sam and Tham - a story of two contrasting entrepreneurs - demonstrated (or lacked) passion and intrinsic drive. And the lessons that can be learnt from their experience.

Step with Key Focuses	Sam and Tham's Implementation Journey
Discover Your Deep Why - Reflect on personal motivations and the purpose behind your entrepreneurial endeavours.	Sam spent time reflecting on his purpose. His "why" was clear: simplifying lives through seamless smart home integration.

- Connect your purpose to your values and life objectives.	Tham was excited by the idea of success but hadn't clarified a personal "why," leading to shallow engagement with each project.
Nurture Genuine Passion - Choose ventures that spark your excitement and curiosity. - Stay connected to what excites you, especially in hard times. - Make your business an expression of your passions.	Sam was genuinely interested in technology, which simplified life. He enjoyed experimenting, coding, and making gadgets better. Tham followed what was trendy but did not have a deep connection with the project. His enthusiasm was short-lived when the novelty wore off.
Build Internal Motivation, Not Just External Validation - Focus on personal growth and mastery. - Let curiosity and purpose drive you, not just money or status. - Measure success by progress, not just external approval.	Sam enjoyed cracking challenging problems and learning along the way. His interest and motivation weren't merely for external validation but for creating something worthwhile. Tham was motivated by extrinsic rewards, such as investor accolades or friends' appreciation. And he was deflated when it did not materialize.
Channel Passion into Consistent Action - Transform enthusiasm into daily habits and routines. - Develop a disciplined approach, even when motivation dips. - Prioritize actions that move you toward your vision.	Sam consistently put in long hours coding and refining his platform. His passion showed in his discipline and follow-through. Tham struggled to sustain effort over time, often abandoning projects halfway through when challenges arose.
Persevere Through Challenges with Purpose	Sam's prototype crashed in front of investors, but his drive pushed him to stay up all night fixing it. He didn't

- View setbacks as opportunities to grow and improve.	give up because he believed in his purpose.
- Lean on your "why" to maintain resilience.	After criticism from an associate about his lack of a business model, Tham doubted himself and gave up entirely on his latest project.
- Keep pushing forward even when results aren't immediate.	
Inspire Others with Your Energy and Commitment - Your passion can ignite motivation in your team and stakeholders. - Lead by example with visible dedication and enthusiasm. - Share your story and mission with conviction.	Sam's excitement was contagious. His unwavering commitment inspired his team and attracted investors who believed in his vision. Tham struggled to rally support because he lacked consistent energy and belief in his ideas.
Stay True to Your Passion While Evolving Your Approach - As you grow, keep your core passion alive, but stay adaptable in strategy. - Revisit and reconnect with your purpose regularly. - Allow your passion to evolve with your experiences.	Sam held quarterly reviews to reassess his goals and strategies, but his core passion remained his anchor. Tham jumped from idea to idea without a clear passion to return to, losing direction along the way.

Key Takeaways:

- Fuel your journey with passion, but let intrinsic drive power your daily actions and long-term focus.
- Stay deeply connected to your purpose; internal motivation sustains you when external rewards fade.
- Show up consistently; genuine passion and purpose inspire others and turn vision into lasting success.

Self-Assessment: Are You Cultivating Passion and Intrinsic Drive?

Rate yourself on each statement from 1 (Never) to 5 (Always):

1. I have a deep connection to my business's mission and purpose.
2. My work excites me and energizes me, even during challenging times.
3. I remain committed to my vision, even when I do not receive validation or rewards from others.
4. Even when I feel less motivated, I persist in taking the necessary actions towards my goals.
5. I work on fully committing to my objectives; Obstacles help me learn, grow, and strengthen my resolve.
6. Passionate people who help me create and fuel my enthusiasm are the ones I want to have around me.
7. To restore energy and focus, I regularly reflect and connect with my purpose - "my why."
8. I make consistent progress toward long-term goals by positively channelling passion with discipline.

Score Interpretation:

- **35-40**: Strong passion and drive - deeply connected to your mission.
- **25-34**: Solid motivation - reconnect with your purpose.
- **15-24**: Revisit your "why" and build habits to reignite passion.
- **Below 15**: At risk of burnout - reset and reclaim your purpose.

Author's Tip: Reconnect with your "why" often. Success doesn't come from fleeting excitement but from sustained, purpose-driven action and unwavering determination.

1.1.4. Confidence and Self-Belief

Confidence and self-belief are not merely individual characteristics but also critical traits necessary for entrepreneurial success. They give you the courage to take risks, overcome doubt, and stay committed to your vision. Even when the odds seem stacked against you, you appear formidable.

Richard Branson, the founder of Virgin Group, embodies this mindset. He didn't simply play it safe with what he knew; he boldly ventured into sectors without any experience and demonstrated that confidence and self-belief were often key to breaking new ground.

When you trust yourself, barriers become stepping stones rather than roadblocks. Self-belief sharpens decision-making, enabling you to trust your instincts, take calculated risks, and convert challenges into opportunities. It also has a ripple effect, as your confidence and self-belief inspire your team, draw investors, and establish trust with customers who can feel your conviction.

Confidence is a business asset that drives innovation, leadership, and expansion. This segment will give you real-world strategies to develop unshakeable confidence so you can boldly step forward, overcome obstacles, and create something truly exceptional.

Let's see how Sam and Tham - a story of two contrasting entrepreneurs, succeeded (or not) in demonstrating confidence and self-belief and what we can learn from their experience.

Steps and Key Focuses	Sam and Tham's Implementation Journey
Celebrate Milestones - Build momentum by recognizing progress. - Reinforce belief in your abilities with regular achievements.	Sam worked on specific and measurable goals to realize his Vision. He celebrated accomplished goals like completing prototypes or securing user feedback. Tham overlooked these milestones, focusing only on distant, unattainable goals.

Practice Positive Self-Talk - Combat self-doubt with affirmations. - Maintain a positive mindset by revisiting past successes.	Sam replaced self-doubt with affirmations like "I'm learning and growing" and kept a journal of accomplishments to revisit during tough times. Tham allowed negative self-talk to paralyze him.
Focus on Continuous Learning - Strengthen competence through expanded knowledge. - Build confidence by mastering new skills.	Sam enrolled in AI courses and attended industry events, consistently improving his skills. Tham hesitated to invest in learning, fearing he wasn't ready.
Visualize a Positive Outcome - Reinforce belief in your potential with visualization exercises. - Mentally prepare for success.	Before every pitch, Sam spent a few minutes visualizing a positive outcome, boosting his confidence and composure. Tham avoided this step, often feeling unprepared.
Accept and Learn from Failure - Turn failures into stepping stones for growth. - Build resilience and confidence by learning from mistakes.	After setbacks, Sam reflected on what went wrong, adjusting his approach with renewed determination. Tham saw failure as a personal flaw and avoided taking further risks.
Practice Confidence-Building Exercises	Sam pushed himself to lead presentations and attend networking events, even when it felt intimidating.

- Develop self-assurance through repeated exposure to challenging situations. - Build courage with consistent practice.	Tham avoided stepping out of his comfort zone and missed growth opportunities.
Focus on Strengths and Unique Qualities - Emphasize what makes you unique. - Approach challenges with confidence in your abilities.	Sam listed his unique strengths - strategic thinking and clear communication - and leaned on them to differentiate himself. Tham struggled to recognise and leverage his talents.

Key Takeaways:

- Take consistent action to build confidence and strengthen self-belief.
- Celebrate small wins to boost momentum and reinforce progress.
- Surround yourself with mentors and supporters to gain courage and inspire trust.

Self-Assessment: Are You Cultivating Confidence and Self-Belief?

Rate yourself on each statement from 1 (Never) to 5 (Always):

1. I set milestones and celebrate small wins to recognise my progress and reinforce confidence.
2. I practice positive self-talk and focus on affirming my strengths.
3. I dedicate time to continuous learning and expanding my knowledge.
4. I visualise success to strengthen my belief in achieving my goals.
5. I maintain a network of supportive people who encourage and motivate me.
6. I view failure as a learning opportunity and use setbacks to grow.
7. I regularly engage in activities that stretch my comfort zone.
8. I focus on my unique strengths and qualities to build self-assurance.

Score Interpretation:

- **35-40**: You face challenges with boldness and motivation.
- **25-34**: Fairly confident; strengthen certain areas of self-belief.
- **15-24**: Confidence is limited. Focus on small wins and positive self-talk to grow belief in yourself.
- **Below 15**: Prioritize building resilience and self-worth immediately

Author's Tip: Build your confidence by embracing challenges as opportunities to grow and trusting your instincts, experience, and information to guide bold decisions.

1.1.5. Grit - Resilience, Perseverance, and Discipline

Talent and intelligence can only take you so far in the entrepreneurial world. What separates those who thrive from those who falter is **Grit** - the powerful combination of **Resilience**, **Perseverance**, and **Discipline**. It's the ability to stay the course, push through setbacks, and keep working towards your goals even when things get tough (and they always do).

Grit isn't about working harder for a few days or weeks; it's about sustained, focused effort over years, sometimes decades. Angela Duckworth, who popularized the concept of grit, describes it as "passion and perseverance for very long-term goals." Entrepreneurs with grit don't give up after the first failure (or the fifth). They find a way forward, learn from every experience, and keep building.

But grit isn't just about endurance. It's about **discipline** - the daily habits and practices that keep you on track. Successful entrepreneurs show up consistently, prioritize what matters, and avoid distractions that pull them away from their mission.

When you combine resilience (the ability to bounce back), perseverance (the drive to keep going), and discipline (the ability to stay focused and organized), you build an unstoppable force.

Let's explore how Sam and Tham, two entrepreneurs with similar potential but very different outcomes, demonstrated (or lacked) grit, and what their journeys teach us.

Step with Key Focuses	Sam and Tham's Implementation Journey
Commit to Long-Term Goals - Develop an unwavering commitment to your vision. - Embrace the fact that success is a marathon, not a sprint. - Stay patient through slow progress.	Sam had a clear vision and was committed to building an integrated smart home platform. Despite setbacks, he knew it was a long-term play and stayed focused for years. Tham jumped from one trendy idea to another, unable to commit to a single goal long enough to see it through.

Build Resilience Through Failure - Accept failure as part of the journey. - Analyze mistakes and bounce back stronger. - Maintain emotional stability under pressure.	Sam faced public failure during his investor demo but used it as fuel to improve his prototype. His ability to stay calm, reflect, and quickly adjust impressed his investors and team. Tham took criticism personally and let failures shake his confidence, eventually abandoning projects.
Maintain Perseverance in Adversity - Push through obstacles and slow periods. - Stay motivated without external validation. - Avoid quitting in the face of rejection or doubt.	Sam persevered through sleepless nights, technical roadblocks, and investor rejections. He kept showing up, refining his product, and finding solutions. Tham lost interest once the initial excitement wore off and struggled to maintain momentum without immediate results.
Exercise Daily Discipline - Stick to routines and productive habits. - Avoid distractions that dilute the focus. - Prioritize tasks that drive progress.	Sam structured his time around clear milestones and daily priorities. He said no to distractions and focused on product development and customer feedback. Tham lacked routine and structure. New ideas constantly pulled his attention away from executing existing projects.
Develop Mental Toughness - Cultivate an unshakeable mindset. - Stay optimistic without being unrealistic. - Remain calm and decisive under pressure.	Sam remained mentally tough, especially when things went wrong. He stayed positive but grounded, making calculated decisions even when under stress. Tham wavered under pressure, second-guessing decisions and

	avoiding tough conversations that could have moved his projects forward.
Track Progress and Stay Accountable - Measure your efforts against your goals. - Review setbacks as learning moments. - Hold yourself accountable to consistent action.	Sam tracked his team's progress and held regular reviews to ensure they were moving toward their vision. He made adjustments based on data and feedback. Tham avoided accountability, often losing track of where his projects stood and failing to evaluate his performance.
Find Strength in Purpose - Let your purpose fuel your resilience. - Align daily actions with your mission. - Use your "why" to sustain motivation during tough times.	Sam found strength in his mission to simplify people's lives through innovative technology. His purpose drove him to keep going, even when it was difficult. Tham lacked a clear purpose, which made it easier for him to give up when things got hard. His projects didn't have a deeper meaning for him.

Key Takeaways:

- Build grit through resilience, perseverance, and disciplined action - this is your ultimate edge.
- Treat failure as feedback; learn, adapt, and keep moving forward.
- Stay focused on your purpose; it fuels the discipline needed for long-term success.

Self-Assessment: Are You Demonstrating Grit (Resilience + Perseverance + Discipline)?

Rate yourself on each statement from 1 (Never) to 5 (Always):

1. I stay committed to my long-term vision, even when progress feels slow or difficult.
2. I bounce back quickly from setbacks or failures, focusing on solutions instead of dwelling on problems.
3. Despite prolonged or delayed results, I always take action.
4. I maintain a disciplined routine that prioritizes my most important tasks every day.
5. I routinely evaluate my progress and modify my plans in light of what is and is not working.
6. I stay focused on one core mission rather than getting distracted by shiny new ideas or trends.
7. I use constructive feedback (even when it's harsh) to re-strategize and enhance my performance.
8. My "why," or purpose, gives me the strength to persevere through difficult times.

Score Interpretation:

- **35-40:** Exceptional grit!
- **25-34:** Strengthen key habits to handle setbacks.
- **15-24:** Build daily discipline and treat setbacks as lessons.
- **Below 15:** Reconnect with your purpose and cultivate resilience through routine.

Author's Tip: Grit fuels success when the exhilaration fades - build resilience, stay consistent, and keep showing up for your vision. Break big goals into daily actions and prioritize what matters most.

Section 1.2: Traits for Navigating Challenges and Opportunities
Case Study: Benny & Penny's Bakehouse: A Recipe for Success

Benny and Penny weren't your typical entrepreneurs. Penny was a meticulous planner, obsessed with colour-coded spreadsheets and precise measurements, while Benny was the kind of person who'd wake up with a wild idea and dive in headfirst - sometimes still in his pyjamas. Together, they ran **Benny & Penny's Bakehouse**, a quirky bakery known for its offbeat, creative pastries, like croissants stuffed with candy bars and cookies baked with surprise fillings. Their tagline? **"Where Sweet Meets Unexpected."** Customers adored their playful approach to baking, but running the business wasn't as simple as whipping up a batch of muffins.

Everything was running smoothly until a supplier delay left them without their signature ingredient for their bestselling **"ChocoBlast Croissant"** for three months. Penny stared at her spreadsheets in horror. "This is a disaster!" she groaned. Benny, unfazed, took a bite of a cinnamon roll. "Relax," he said. "We'll just make something new in the meantime. Something spicy."

That's how the **"Flamin' Hot Brownie"** was born - a rich, fudgy brownie with a fiery chilli kick. Penny wasn't convinced, but Benny was already sketching the recipe on a napkin. She sighed, updated her spreadsheets, and reached out to their suppliers. To her surprise, the new product was an instant hit. Customers couldn't get enough of the unexpected sweet-and-spicy combination, proving that sometimes, a little spontaneity and willingness to experiment could work wonders.

But not all of Benny's ideas were winners. One morning, he declared, "We should launch a **'Bakehouse for Pets'** line. Treats for cats and dogs! Imagine the market!" Penny folded her arms. "Have you ever met a cat? They turn their noses up at the finest gourmet meals, let alone a pumpkin pup-cake." Benny shrugged. "Risk is part of the game! We won't know unless we try."

Penny, who preferred calculated risks over Benny's "throw sprinkles at the wall and see what sticks" approach, agreed to a small test run. It bombed - hilariously. Social media was flooded with pictures of unimpressed pets sitting beside untouched treats. Penny shook her head while Benny laughed. "At least we learned something! Data is data," he grinned, already brainstorming the next idea.

Their biggest challenge came at a major food expo, where they planned to secure café and grocery store partnerships. As they were setting up their booth, Benny froze. "Uh… we have a problem," he admitted. Penny turned slowly. "What kind of problem?"

"The we-forgot-half-our-display-samples kind of problem."

Penny nearly lost it. "How do you forget the actual product?" she snapped. Benny, ever resourceful, quickly improvised. He turned their booth into a **"Create Your Own Pastry"** station, inviting attendees to sketch their dream desserts. By the end of the day, they had dozens of pre-orders for custom pastries and a long list of interested retailers. Penny had to admit - Benny's ability to turn disasters into opportunities was impressive.

But it wasn't all about Benny's last-minute ideas. Penny's ability to take the initiative kept their bakery running smoothly behind the scenes. When she noticed ingredient costs rising, she didn't wait for Benny to realize. She found a new supplier, negotiated discounts for bulk purchases, and even obtained free samples for product testing. When Benny finally looked at their financial reports and noticed their enhanced margins, he raised an eyebrow. "Wait, how did we do that?" Penny grinned and pushed a spreadsheet across the counter.

Marketing their bakehouse also needed some creative magic. As sales reached a plateau, Penny recommended that they do an interactive **"Battle of the Bakes"** on Instagram, where customers could vote on wild and wacky pastry concepts like the **Peanut Butter Pretzel Croissant** or the **Gothic Chocolate Lava Cake**. Benny went even further, donning a **"Pastry Gladiator"** costume and recording over-the-top skits where the pastries "battled" each other for a spot on the menu. The campaign went viral, their customer base increased overnight, and they sold out of several flavours within days.

By the end of their second year in the business, Benny and Penny had experienced it all - supply chain disasters, product launch failures, surprise successes, and even a customer who sent them a photo of a raccoon stealing a pilfered pastry. Along the way, they discovered that the skills of adapting, taking risks, getting creative, finding solutions on the fly, and stepping up weren't just useful - they were necessary.

Sitting in their bakery one afternoon, Benny rocked back in his chair, munching on a cookie. "You know," he said, "we make a pretty good team. You keep us from going out of business, and I keep us from being boring." Penny rolled her eyes but smiled. "Let's just agree - no more pet pastries."

Benny smiled. "Okay, okay. But listen, how about a **Taco Croissant**?"

Penny sighed. "Why do I even bother?"

Their journey was far from over, but one thing was sure - as long as Penny had her spreadsheets and Benny had his bold and crazy ideas, they'd find a way to keep the adventure going.

1.2.1. Adaptability and Flexibility

Being adaptable and flexible is really important in today's fast-moving business world. The best entrepreneurs are those who can adapt their strategy and plans as needed, based on research, data, and results, and adjust to new situations. For example, Slack started as a gaming company but evolved into one of the most popular tools for teamwork by adapting well.

Being flexible is being open to change, anticipating its impact, staying agile, and turning challenges into opportunities. Adaptable entrepreneurs don't just survive changes in the market but find ways to benefit from them and fuel growth. When markets change, technology evolves, and customer needs change, they embrace uncertainty, refine their plans as needed, and keep up with customers' wants. Those who can adapt to these changes will do well.

In this segment, we'll look at ways to help you become more flexible and adaptable. Adjusting while staying strong is key to growing and innovating in business, not just getting by.

Thriving Through Change: How Benny & Penny Mastered Adaptability

Benny and Penny's journey running their quirky bakehouse is a perfect example of how adaptability and flexibility shape a business's success. Whether embracing bold ideas or tackling unexpected challenges, their ability (or occasional reluctance) to pivot helped them build a resilient and innovative bakery.

Let's explore how Benny and Penny demonstrated adaptability and flexibility, and the lessons we can learn from their journey.

Steps with Key Focuses	Benny & Penny's Implementation Journey
Stay Informed About Market Trends and Customer Needs	Penny routinely tracked baking trends and sent out customer surveys to understand preferences.

- Proactively gather insights to stay ahead. - Make informed, data-driven decisions.	Benny, always in the middle of conversations, stayed ahead of competitors by chatting with customers on social media and keenly watching emerging food fads.
Adopt a Learning Mindset - Approach challenges with curiosity. - Commit to continuous learning and professional development.	Benny saw every obstacle as a chance to innovate (even if it meant experimenting with Taco Croissants). Penny, an ever-evolving individual, enrolled in advanced pastry workshops to refine techniques and expand their menu.
Test and Scale - Foster innovation through controlled experiments. - Minimize risk while testing new ideas.	Benny championed small-scale tests like the *Flamin' Hot Brownie*, gathering customer feedback before committing to a full rollout. Penny carefully analyzed the results, ensuring recipes and pricing were optimized before a large-scale launch.
Seek Feedback and Listen to Your Team - Leverage diverse perspectives to identify opportunities. - Address concerns with collaborative solutions.	Penny organised weekly meetings to gather staff insights, ensuring their voices were heard. Benny, always open to spontaneity, encouraged anonymous feedback, knowing that sometimes the wildest ideas turned into their biggest hits.
Create Contingency Plans - Prepare for uncertainty with alternative strategies. - Use scenario planning to mitigate risks.	Penny developed detailed contingency plans for ingredient shortages and pricing fluctuations, ensuring they never faced another *ChocoBlast Croissant* disaster unprepared. While more spontaneous, Benny began to appreciate the value of

	backup plans, especially after many entrepreneurs showed up to a major trade show without products.
Build a Culture of Flexibility - Empower teams to adapt collaboratively. - Foster a culture of innovation and adaptability.	Benny encouraged staff to pitch creative pastry ideas, rewarding innovation and spontaneity. Penny introduced structured training programs to strengthen problem-solving skills and ensure the team could easily handle high-pressure situations.
Evaluate and Adjust Regularly - Stay responsive to market shifts. - Continuously refine strategies based on performance metrics.	Penny conducted monthly financial and product performance reviews, ensuring their menu stayed profitable and aligned with customer demand. Benny's last-minute experiments often benefited from his structured, data-driven insights.
Stay Aligned to Your Vision but Open to Change - Balance long-term vision with flexibility to evolve. - Adapt methods while staying true to core goals.	While Penny focused on maintaining the bakehouse's core mission of "comfort food with a twist," Benny pushed for unconventional, attention-grabbing innovations - like the wildly successful *Battle of the Bakes* marketing campaign.

Key Takeaways:

- Stay adaptable - pivot quickly to seize new opportunities and navigate change.
- Be flexible - embrace innovation and solve problems proactively to stay competitive.
- Combine strategy with creativity - embrace challenges, learn fast, and stay ready for what's next.

Self-Assessment: Are You Cultivating Adaptability and Flexibility?

Rate yourself on each statement from 1 (Never) to 5 (Always):

1. I stay informed about market trends, customer needs, and industry changes.
2. I maintain a growth mindset and view challenges as opportunities for learning.
3. I encourage experimentation and test new ideas on a small scale.
4. I seek and listen to feedback from team members and customers.
5. I have contingency plans in place for unexpected challenges.
6. I foster a culture of flexibility and innovation within my team.
7. I regularly evaluate and adjust my strategies to align with current conditions.
8. I stay committed to my vision while remaining open to adapting my approach.

Score Interpretation:

- **35-40**: You demonstrate flexibility and responsiveness to change.
- **25-34**: Targeted improvements can enhance your adaptability.
- **15-24**: Focus on growth mindset, feedback, and regular reflection.
- **Below 15**: Prioritize developing adaptability and openness to change.

Author's Tip: Embrace adaptability as your superpower. Stay open to change, pivot when necessary, and turn challenges into opportunities.

1.2.2. Risk-Taking

The underlying spirit of entrepreneurship is about taking risks, seizing opportunities, and having the courage to push boundaries. But risk-taking is not gambling. Instead, making the right strategic and informed decisions at the right time, taking the opportunity and opening doors to success.

Take Daniel Georg Ek, co-founder of Spotify, as an example. He challenged the existing norms of the music industry and completely transformed how we consume music. How did he manage to do that? He made an informed decision and leaped with conviction towards his Vision.

Risk-takers like him consistently outperform their competition by taking calculated risks and making good business decisions. They know what note to hit to create waves, overcome obstacles, and diversify their markets.

Risk-taking also has a multiplier effect. It attracts success, draws the best talent, inspires confidence in investors, and pulls in customers. Playing it safe will keep the business afloat, but it won't make it stand out, nor will you leave a lasting legacy.

This segment will give you practical strategies for assessing and embracing risk to take necessary actions that lead to long-term growth and differentiate you in the market.

The Art of Smart Risks: Benny & Penny's Bakehouse

At Benny & Penny's Bakehouse, Benny and Penny's journey was a wild ride filled with audacious choices, measured risks, and the occasional leap of faith, trying not to inadvertently cross the fine line between strategic bravery and reckless decisions. While Benny thrived on intuition and gut instinct, Penny insisted on structure, data, and contingency plans. A balance of bold ideas and thoughtful planning helped the bakery flourish.

Let's examine Benny and Penny's risk-taking behaviours and the lessons we can draw from their experience.

Step and Key Focuses	Benny & Penny's Implementation Journey
Define Your Risk Tolerance - Balance ambition with a realistic understanding of limits. - Use risk tolerance as a guide for decision-making.	Penny carefully assessed their financial and operational limits before agreeing to Benny's Taco Croissant experiment. Though eager to try anything, Benny learned to trust Penny's analysis to avoid overstretching their resources.
Conduct Thorough Research - Reduce uncertainty with preparation. - Base decisions on evidence and insights.	Penny conducted customer surveys and studied seasonal food trends before launching their Battle of the Bakes campaign. Benny, who usually relied on gut instinct, learned the value of research - especially after the pet pastry flop.
Evaluate Potential Outcomes and Impact - Anticipate consequences to make informed decisions. - Assess how outcomes align with business goals.	When Benny suggested offering mystery flavour pastries, Penny mapped out best-case, worst-case, and likely scenarios. Benny's approach - "What's the worst that could happen?" - was far less structured, but he appreciated Penny's strategic foresight.
Use a Cost-Benefit Analysis - Align risks with long-term business value.	Before approving Benny's idea for neon-coloured pastry boxes, Penny calculated costs and potential brand impact. Benny, ever optimistic, pushed for the bold branding move, ultimately maximizing returns through viral marketing.

- Weigh potential rewards against resource investments.	
Start with Low-Stakes Experiments - Test ideas on a small scale to refine them before scaling. - Use controlled experiments to manage risk.	Benny's limited-time Flamin' Hot Brownie and Penny's one-store pilot for a DIY (Do It Yourself) Cookie Kit allowed them to test ideas before fully committing, minimizing potential losses.
Track Performance vs. Milestones - Keep efforts focused on measurable goals. - Identify when to pivot or double down.	Penny set revenue and customer feedback goals for their new seasonal flavours. Benny preferred celebrating over tracking but appreciated the milestones after seeing how they helped optimize product launches.
Develop Contingency Plans - Reduce stress by preparing for unexpected setbacks. - Enable quick, effective responses to challenges.	Penny created backup plans for ingredient shortages and unexpected shipment delays. Benny, who initially resisted planning for "what-ifs," quickly saw the value when a trade show mishap forced them to pivot their entire presentation on the spot.

Build Resilience	Benny saw every mistake - like burned pastries or the failed pet treats - as an opportunity to improve. "Next time, more cinnamon!" he'd say.
- Embrace challenges as opportunities for growth.	
- Develop the courage to learn from failures.	Penny is more cautious, adjusts strategies with each failure, and learns to adapt rather than panic.

Key Takeaways:

- Take smart, calculated risks - pair bold moves with preparation and market insight.
- Balance fearless execution with thoughtful planning to turn risks into growth opportunities.
- Stay flexible and adaptable - turn challenges into creative wins and keep moving forward.

Self-Assessment: Are You Embracing Calculated Risks?

Rate yourself on each statement from 1 (Never) to 5 (Always):

1. I understand my risk tolerance and take risks that align with it.
2. I thoroughly research potential risks before committing to them.
3. I evaluate both positive and negative outcomes of a risk before proceeding.
4. I use cost-benefit analysis to weigh the value of taking a risk.
5. I start with low-stakes experiments to test new ideas and minimize loss.
6. I set clear objectives and milestones when taking a risk to track progress.
7. I have contingency plans to manage setbacks if a risk doesn't work out.
8. I view failures as learning opportunities and cultivate resilience.

Score Interpretation:

- **35-40**: You take calculated risks while managing the downsides.
- **25-34**: Strengthening key areas can boost your confidence and decision-making.
- **15-24**: Focus on research, planning, and small experiments to improve your risk strategy.
- **Below 15**: You may be missing key opportunities - start building a mindset for calculated risk-taking now.

 Author's Tip: Calculated risks are stepping stones to innovation and growth. Assess the potential rewards and make informed decisions. Remember, strategic bold moves don't just drive success - they set you apart in a crowded market.

1.2.3. Creativity and Innovation

What makes certain companies change and even disrupt existing industry norms or ways of providing products and services? Creativity helps come up with new ideas, while innovation focuses on putting those ideas into action and creating real solutions that reshape industries.

Take Airbnb, for example. Its founders didn't invent hospitality; they reimagined it. By thinking differently about how people find places to stay, they disrupted an entire industry and created a global movement. That's the power of combining creativity with innovation.

Businesses that innovate start trends instead of just following them. They sell special products, services, and experiences that captivate customers and build lasting loyalty. Innovation allows them to stay ahead of change, whether adapting to new technology, responding to shifting consumer needs or developing more efficient ways to operate. Moreover, creative problem-solving turns obstacles into opportunities, helping businesses discover new revenue streams and competitive advantages.

In today's fast-paced world, you'll get left behind if you don't keep moving forward. In this segment, we will discuss integrating creativity and innovation in your business so you can succeed and stay ahead.

Igniting Creativity and Driving Innovation at Benny & Penny's Bakehouse

Benny & Penny's Bakehouse didn't become a success through the use of conventional recipes. Their ability to embrace creativity and foster innovation distinguished them in a competitive market crowded with pastries and confections. Though their individual styles tended to come into conflict - Penny preferred disciplined creativity, while Benny lived on capricious moments of inspiration - they showed that innovation is not necessarily about grand ideas; it's about incorporating those ideas into practical, game-changing solutions.

Let's discuss how Benny and Penny showed creativity and innovation and what we can learn from their experience.

Steps and Key Focuses	Benny & Penny's Implementation Journey
Encourage a Culture of Curiosity - Foster curiosity with questions that challenge norms. - Stay informed about trends and innovations.	Benny constantly asked, "What if we turned this pastry into something completely unexpected?" - This led to creations like the *Flamin' Hot Brownie* and *Peanut Butter Pretzel Croissant.* Meanwhile, Penny stayed on top of food trends and baking innovations, ensuring they stayed ahead of the curve.
Engage in Brainstorming Sessions - Generate diverse solutions through open dialogue. - Create an environment where all ideas are welcome.	Penny scheduled weekly brainstorming sessions where the team could contribute ideas. She relied on whiteboards and sticky notes to structure discussions, while Benny's free-flowing style turned these meetings into high-energy creative sessions. Some ideas, like the *DIY Baking Kit,* came from these lively debates.
Use Creative Problem-Solving Techniques - Approach challenges from fresh angles. - Use structured techniques to encourage innovation.	When their workflow became inefficient, Penny applied design thinking to optimize processes. On the other hand, Benny leaned into lateral thinking - like when he suggested pastry delivery via drones (which Penny tactfully vetoed). Instead, she introduced a pre-order system that improved efficiency.

Seek Inspiration Beyond Your Industry - Borrow concepts from other industries. - Adapt successful ideas to fit your business model.	Penny drew inspiration from fine dining and retail experiences, implementing an "open kitchen" concept where customers could watch their pastries bake. Benny looked to street food vendors, inspiring on-the-go snack pastries that became a bestseller.
Test Your Idea - Validate ideas through low-cost, small-scale trials. - Gather insights to improve before scaling up.	Benny loved launching new pastries, but Penny insisted on small-scale testing first. Introducing *Croissant Cone Sundae* to a small group of loyal customers before rolling out storewide. Feedback from the launch helped refine the product, ensuring a smoother launch.
Learn From Failures - Transform setbacks into opportunities for growth. - Use lessons from failures to improve future projects.	Their "Pet Pastry" experiment flopped, with unimpressed cats refusing to touch the treats. Benny found it hilarious. "At least we learned something! Data is data!" Penny documented the failure to refine future product testing methods.
Surround Yourself with Diverse Perspectives - Leverage diversity to spark unique ideas. - Actively seek input from a range of experiences and backgrounds.	Their team included bakers, marketers, and tech-savvy interns, fostering a melting pot of ideas. Penny valued structured customer feedback, while Benny's networking skills helped bring fresh insights from fellow entrepreneurs.
Maintain a Growth Mindset - Embrace challenges as opportunities to learn.	Penny took business courses to sharpen her strategic thinking, while Benny's creative writing class

- Continuously seek experiences that expand creativity.	inspired fun product names like *"Cone of Destiny"* and *"Lava Love Cake."* Their commitment to learning fueled constant innovation.

Key Takeaways:

- Experiment with unique ideas to drive differentiation by taking risks and innovating to stand out.
- Balance solid planning with bold creativity to turn fresh ideas into practical results.
- Leverage diverse perspectives to fuel continuous learning and inspire innovation.

Self-Assessment: Are You Cultivating Creativity and Innovation?

Rate yourself on each statement from 1 (Never) to 5 (Always):

1. I regularly explore new ideas, trends, and technologies that could inspire innovation.
2. I engage in brainstorming sessions to generate fresh ideas and encourage open discussion.
3. I use creative problem-solving techniques to find unique solutions to challenges.
4. I seek inspiration from industries outside my own to bring in new perspectives.
5. I experiment and create prototypes to test ideas on a small scale.
6. I view failure as a learning tool and analyze setbacks to improve future efforts.
7. I surround myself with diverse perspectives that encourage creative thinking.
8. I maintain a growth mindset that welcomes new challenges and learning opportunities.

Score Interpretation:

- **35-40**: Your approach supports fresh, unique solutions that drive growth and adaptability.
- **25-34**: Addressing specific areas can help improve your ability to generate and apply innovative ideas.
- **15-24**: Focusing on brainstorming, experimentation, and diverse perspectives will strengthen your capacity for innovation.
- **Below 15**: Immediate attention to building a creative and innovative mindset is recommended.

Author's Tip: The best ideas often come from questioning what others take for granted. Stay curious, experiment boldly, and let thoughtful creativity guide you toward innovative solutions that redefine possibilities.

1.2.4. Resourcefulness

One of the core tenets of business is the optimum utilization of what you have, including time, finance, people and opportunities. Resourcefulness is finding innovative ways to optimize all resources by making and finding creative solutions and implementing wise strategic decisions, especially when challenges arise. It's what separates those who thrive from those who struggle when faced with limited funding, small teams, or unexpected hurdles.

A great example is Michele Romanow. While in college, she opened a coffee shop that focused on being good for the environment. Then, she started a company called Buytopia with little money and grew it to make millions by teaming up with others and keeping things simple. Later, she helped create Clearco, which offers an innovative way to fund e-commerce businesses. She has the ability to spot significant opportunities and showcases resourcefulness at its finest.

Being resourceful isn't just about saving money; it's about thinking differently. It encourages people to solve problems creatively, find hidden opportunities, and build sustainable businesses without overextending themselves. It also fosters adaptability, helping business owners pivot when needed and maintain momentum despite scarce resources.

The good news is that anyone can learn to be more resourceful. In this segment, we'll share easy tips to help you do more with less, run your business better, and create a business that can keep going strong no matter what challenges come up.

Resourcefulness Unleashed at Benny & Penny's Bakehouse

Benny & Penny's Bakehouse's success resulted from their knack for making each dollar go farther, being clever, and using limitations as advantages. From negotiating favourable terms from suppliers to designing viral marketing programs on a shoestring budget, Benny and Penny excelled in doing more for less.

Let us examine how Benny and Penny exemplified resourcefulness and the lessons we may learn from them.

Steps with Key Focuses	Benny & Penny's Implementation Journey
Set Clear Priorities - Allocate resources to high-impact activities. - Align efforts with key business objectives.	Penny ensured their limited budget focused on what mattered most - producing high-quality pastries and keeping customers happy. She cut unnecessary costs and optimized spending. Benny found creative ways to support these priorities, often experimenting with low-cost but high-impact marketing ideas.
Leverage Free or Low-Cost Tools - Enhance efficiency while minimizing costs. - Use budget-friendly tools to streamline operations.	Penny used free and budget-friendly project management tools to streamline team collaboration and keep track of orders. Benny scouted free design templates to create eye-catching flyers and social media graphics without hiring a professional.
Seek Out Partnerships and Collaborations - Expand resources through strategic partnerships. - Increase visibility without significant spending.	Benny partnered with a local coffee shop to feature their pastries, expanding their customer base without extra marketing costs. Penny collaborated with food bloggers and micro-influencers, trading delicious treats for exposure instead of paying for ads.
Embrace DIY ("Do It Yourself") Solutions When Possible	Benny managed their social media, crafting witty posts and engaging directly with customers instead of hiring a digital agency.

- Save money while gaining hands-on experience. - Build a deeper understanding of business functions.	Penny handled essential website updates herself, avoiding outsourcing fees while ensuring their branding stayed on point.
Negotiate and Compare Options - Make informed, budget-friendly decisions. - Use negotiation to maximize value.	Penny secured better rates with suppliers by negotiating bulk orders and long-term contracts, saving money without sacrificing quality. Benny researched multiple delivery service providers for the most cost-effective yet reliable option.
Repurpose and Reuse Resources - Maximize the value of existing resources. - Reduce waste through creative repurposing.	Penny ensured that leftover croissant dough didn't go to waste - she turned it into bite-sized pastry samples that customers could try for free, leading to more sales. Benny repurposed content from their blog into email newsletters and engaging Instagram posts, maximizing reach without extra effort.
Cultivate a Mindset of Problem-Solving - Approach challenges with creativity and curiosity. - Turn limitations into growth opportunities.	When their oven broke down during peak hours, Benny quickly adapted, launching a limited-time "No-Bake Dessert Special" that turned a near disaster into a fun and unexpected experience. Penny, always the strategist, applied design thinking to improve their production efficiency and streamline daily operations.
Engage with Relevant Groups - Seek knowledge and support.	Penny joined local entrepreneur groups, gaining valuable business insights and networking with other

- **Leverage relationships for cost-effective solutions.**	bakery owners for supplier recommendations.
	Benny attended food festivals, conversing with vendors and picking up fresh ideas for their next innovative pastry creation.

Key Takeaways:

- Maximize impact by using free tools, synergizing with partners, and repurposing resources - constantly honing your resourcefulness.
- Turn every constraint into an opportunity for innovation and creative problem-solving.
- Collaborate with local businesses and networks to expand reach without overspending.

Self-Assessment: Are You Cultivating Resourcefulness?

Rate yourself on each statement from 1 (Never) to 5 (Always):

1. I set clear priorities and focus resources on the most critical areas.
2. I regularly seek out free or low-cost tools to improve efficiency.
3. I explore partnerships and collaborations to expand my resources.
4. I use DIY solutions to manage tasks whenever possible to save costs.
5. I negotiate and compare options before making purchases.
6. I repurpose and reuse resources to minimize unnecessary expenses.
7. I view challenges as opportunities to find creative solutions.
8. I maintain a strong network that provides guidance and support.

Score Interpretation:

- **35-40**: Highly resourceful. You use strategies that drive sustainable growth and maximize resources.
- **25-34**: Improve specific areas to boost resourcefulness and do more with less.
- **15-24**: Focus on cost-saving tools, synergetic partnerships, and creative problem-solving.
- **Below 15**: Prioritize the development of a resourceful mindset to reduce inefficiencies and reliance on others.

Author's Tip: Resourcefulness is the art of turning limitations into opportunities. Consider constraints as catalysts for creativity, and focus on maximizing the potential of what you already have.

1.2.5. Ability to Take Initiative

Successful businesspeople don't wait for the right moment - they make it. Taking initiative distinguishes those who make ideas a reality from those who merely dream. It's about acting, experimenting with ideas, and taking advantage of opportunities rather than waiting for ideal conditions.

The Canva founders reflect this attitude. Rather than seeking approval, Melanie Perkins took action by designing a straightforward online design program and pitching it to investors after being initially rejected. Taking that first step created a platform for global design. Her experience shows that initiative is not about knowing all the answers; it's about taking the initial step and finding your way toward your objective in the process.

In business, waiting can be expensive. The business world is fast-paced, and opportunities go to those who dare to seize them. Taking initiative allows you to learn through action, refine while doing, test your ideas against tangible feedback, and gain momentum. Progress at each step reinforces your confidence, resilience, and ability to adapt, essential traits for navigating the unpredictable nature of business.

Hesitation can lead to stagnation. Over-planning becomes a never-ending cycle of "almost ready" rather than actual progress. Fear of imperfection can keep you stuck while others move ahead, turning uncertainty into opportunity. Even worse, inaction erodes confidence, making it even more difficult to make strong decisions in the future.

The truth is that action conquers perfection every time. Taking initiative is the driving force that makes ideas real, uncertainty blooms into growth, and people become entrepreneurs. The following segment will give you practical tips for taking the required initiatives, gaining momentum, and getting things done - because success belongs to those who pursue it.

From Ideas to Action: How Benny & Penny's Bakehouse Turned Vision into Reality

Taking initiative was not a choice at Benny & Penny's Bakehouse - it was the key ingredient in their recipe for success. Benny, the spontaneous creator, was never short of ideas, always willing to act without delay. The meticulous planner Penny ensured their energy was channelled into systematic action. Their combination of creativity and planning turned their bakery into a neighbourhood hotspot, demonstrating that innovative ideas require a plan to become a reality.

Let us see how Benny and Penny exhibited the ability to take initiative and the lessons we can draw from their experiences.

Steps with Key Focuses	Benny & Penny's Implementation Journey
Break Down Big Goals into Small Steps - Reduce the overwhelming feeling by creating clear, actionable steps. - Maintain focus on incremental progress.	When Benny devised the idea for a "Midnight Snack Attack" event - a late-night bakery pop-up - Penny divided the work into manageable tasks. She created staffing, supply prep, and social media promotion checklists to ensure a smooth launch.
Set Deadlines to Create Urgency - Create urgency to encourage timely action. - Minimize procrastination with specific milestones.	Benny's impulsive announcement of the event forced the team to act quickly, drumming up excitement. Penny, ever the organizer, set internal deadlines to keep the chaos under control and ensure everything was ready on time.
Start with a Minimum Viable Product (MVP) - Minimize risks with small-scale testing. - Gain insights to refine and improve your offering.	Their DIY Cookie Kit was a pilot project to get customer feedback that helped them tweak the concept before rolling it out across locations, reducing risk while ensuring success.
Adopt a "Fail Fast, Learn Faster" Mindset - Treat failures as feedback.	Benny's "try it and see what happens" approach led to quick lessons - like when an experimental pastry flopped, but the feedback inspired a new recipe that became a

- Act quickly and adjust based on real-world results.	bestseller. Penny documented these lessons to improve future projects.
Focus on Progress Over Perfection - Build momentum by prioritizing completion. - Avoid delays caused by over-analysis or perfectionism.	Penny knew that waiting for perfection could delay opportunities. She initially opted for simple packaging when launching their cookie kits, allowing them to ride the trend while refining details later.
Keep Eyes on the Prize - Boost motivation by focusing on positive possibilities. - Reinforce confidence in taking the first step.	Benny had a knack for rallying the team by vividly portraying success, whether it was customers lining up for their new pastries or the bakery becoming a community favourite.
Seek Accountability - Reinforce commitment with regular check-ins. - Stay on track with accountability systems.	Penny introduced weekly team meetings to track progress, aligning everyone on the new initiatives and responsibilities.
Build on Past Successes - Draw inspiration from previous wins. - Use past successes to boost confidence in new initiatives.	When planning the sequel to their Midnight Snack Attack event, Penny and Benny analyzed what worked in the first event, keeping the best elements while refining the details for an even bigger turnout.

Key Takeaways:

- Take initiative - small actions create momentum and turn ideas into real opportunities.
- Balance bold ideas with structured execution to turn creativity into successful outcomes.
- Embrace "fail fast, learn faster" - test, adapt, and continuously improve for better results.

Self-Assessment: Are You Taking Initiative?

Rate yourself on each statement from 1 (Never) to 5 (Always):

1. I break down big goals into small, manageable steps to encourage action.
2. I set deadlines for tasks and milestones to create a sense of urgency.
3. I develop a minimum viable product (MVP) to test ideas quickly.
4. I view failure as part of the learning process and embrace a "fail fast, learn faster" mindset.
5. I focus on making progress rather than waiting for perfect conditions.
6. I visualize positive outcomes to build motivation and overcome hesitations.
7. I seek accountability by sharing my goals with a mentor or peer group.
8. I reflect on past successes to reinforce my confidence in taking action.

Score Interpretation:

- **35-40:** You move from ideas to action with confidence.
- **25-34:** Targeted improvements can boost your follow-through.
- **15-24:** Strengthen planning, deadlines, and a growth mindset.
- **Below 15:** At risk of inaction. Take steps to overcome hesitation.

Author's Tip: Taking initiative transforms hesitation into momentum and turns fleeting opportunities into lasting success. Be willing to navigate uncertainty, test bold ideas, and take the first step.

Section 1.3: Traits for Building & Sustaining a Thriving Business

Case Study: Rolling With Strength, Strategy, and Success

Ram and Cam were an unlikely duo running a thriving personal health and body training business called "Super Wellness Atelier." What started as a single boutique fitness studio, combining Cam's expertise in strength training with Ram's background in biomechanics and injury prevention, had grown into a multi-location brand that redefined the fitness experience. Their specialty? A hybrid training method that fused high-performance training with cutting-edge recovery techniques, helping clients not just get fit but stay resilient. Their clients swore by it, claiming it had helped them overcome chronic pain, gain confidence, and even conquer their first triathlon. However, scaling their business wasn't as simple as adjusting resistance bands; the duo had much to learn.

Cam was the early riser, often in the gym before dawn, tracking client progress and optimizing workout routines. On the other hand, Ram did his best work late at night, tweaking recovery protocols and testing new wearable tech for performance tracking. "You know, Ram," Cam joked one morning while rolling out his shoulders, "I'm the heart of this operation, and you're the brain". Ram smirked while reviewing a new AI-powered mobility assessment. "And you're the guy who once thought deadlifts before coffee was a good idea." They both laughed, but Cam's relentless drive kept clients motivated while Ram's growth mindset ensured their training programs were constantly evolving.

Their success in their first location was no accident; it was built on an unwavering commitment to their clients and the community. Ram and Cam knew that offering just another gym experience wouldn't cut it. They designed a personalized, holistic training approach that incorporated injury prevention, mobility work, and tailored workout plans. Their clients didn't just train; they became part of a supportive ecosystem that encouraged long-term wellness.

To make their first location a success, they leveraged strategic partnerships. Cam connected with local nutritionists and chiropractors, offering joint wellness packages that provided a full-body approach to health. Ram worked tirelessly on refining their training methods, developing data-driven assessments to measure clients' progress and prevent injuries. This attention to detail and commitment to personalized service quickly set them apart from competitors. Within the first year, Super Wellness Atelier had a waitlist for new clients, and their word-of-mouth referrals skyrocketed.

It wasn't just their expertise that kept Super Wellness Atelier growing. They could network like professionals. Cam was known for making friends with gym equipment suppliers and local physical therapists, securing deals on state-of-the-art gear, and establishing partnerships for client referrals. Meanwhile, Ram was the face of the brand, landing guest appearances on fitness podcasts and getting influencers to swear by their recovery techniques. At a wellness expo, Ram even managed to get a celebrity athlete to try their infrared sauna. Super Wellness Atelier's bookings jumped overnight when she posted about it. "See?" Ram said smugly. "That's how you flex." Cam rolled his eyes but secretly appreciated his partner's flair for building connections.

Their real magic, however, was their obsession with their clients. When a regular customer mentioned that traditional HIIT (High-Intensity Interval Training) workouts aggravate her knee pain, Cam designed a low-impact alternative that still delivered results. When a client training for a marathon needed better sleep, Ram introduced a data-driven recovery protocol using wearable sleep trackers and breathwork exercises. "What's next?" Cam teased. "A program that guarantees six-pack abs and inner peace?" Ram didn't miss a beat. "If it sells, why not?"

Behind the scenes, though, they faced challenges. Ram's approach to finances was to "invest in the experience" (which once meant splurging on a cryotherapy chamber without consulting the budget). Cam, horrified, took it upon himself to ensure they had a solid financial foundation. "Ram, we can't just 'vibe' our way through cash flow management," Cam groaned one afternoon while reviewing expenses. Ram looked unconvinced. "But we can vibe our way through a good recovery session." Still, Cam's insistence on proper financial tracking and smart reinvestment saved them, especially when expansion costs started piling up.

Their long-term vision set them apart. While Ram often dreamed of launching a fitness app, Cam kept them focused on perfecting their in-person client experience first. "Quality over quantity," Cam reminded Ram every time a flashy new idea came up. Ram was convinced after watching a competitor launch too many online programs too fast and collapse under poor customer service and retention. "Okay, fine," Ram admitted, "but when we're ready, I'm calling the app 'Peak Anywhere.'" Cam sighed. "Let's get through this expansion first, genius."

Their complementary strengths helped them navigate the challenges of running a rapidly growing fitness brand and kept the journey exciting. Cam's hands-on coaching style and relentless client focus perfectly matched Ram's innovation and strategic thinking. While their personalities often clashed, Ram once tried to expense a hyperbaric oxygen chamber for "research," Cam nearly deducted it from his paycheck, but they knew they were stronger together.

One evening, as they wrapped up a long day, Cam sat on a bench press, shaking his head. "You know, Ram," he said, "we might just be the perfect training plan. You're the data and recovery, keeping us efficient, and I'm the sweat and grind, pushing us forward." Ram smirked. "And you're also the one who forgets to stretch after workouts." Cam laughed, tossing a resistance band toward him. "Fair enough. But admit it, you'd be bored without me." Ram paused. "Maybe. But don't push your luck."

As Super Wellness Atelier continued to grow, Ram and Cam proved that discipline, customer-centric innovation, financial acumen, networking, and a shared long-term vision weren't just good business traits; they were the pillars of sustained success. And maybe, just maybe, they were the perfect training duo that would keep raising the bar.

1.3.1. Strong Work Ethic

Starting and growing a business takes more than a great idea - it requires relentless dedication, long hours, and a willingness to push through challenges. A strong work ethic separates those who succeed from those who stall. It's about showing up daily, putting in the effort, and staying committed even when progress feels slow.

Entrepreneurs like Robert Herjavec, founder of the Herjavec Group and investor on Shark Tank, exemplify what it means to build success through sheer determination and a relentless work ethic. Starting with little more than ambition and hustle, he took on multiple jobs, taught himself the tech industry, and launched his company from his basement. His rise wasn't all about vision; it was about outworking everybody consistently, doing whatever it took, and never expecting success to come without effort.

A good work ethic fuels resilience, enabling you to power through obstacles instead of being stopped by them, keeps you focused when distractions arise and motivated when setbacks occur. More than professional success, it also sets the tone for your team - when others see your work ethic, it creates a climate of productivity and accountability.

Even the most promising ventures can falter without a strong work ethic, progress becomes inconsistent, obstacles overwhelm, and valuable opportunities fall through the cracks. Entrepreneurial success isn't merely about working hard; it's about working purposefully, consistently, and pushing forward even when the road gets tough.

This segment offers practical strategies to help you strengthen your work ethic, stay focused, and transform your ambition into long-term success.

Rolling With Success

Ram and Cam's experience in developing Super Wellness Atelier exemplified the unyielding value of a strong work ethic. Though their personalities could hardly be more different, Ram flourished on structure and analytics. At the same time, Cam relied on hands-on coaching and big-energy motivation. Their mutual passion for hard work drove them toward success.

Let us see how Ram & Cam demonstrated strong work ethics and what we can learn from their experience.

Steps & Key Focuses	Ram & Cam's implementation journey
Create a Consistent Schedule - Build discipline through routine. - Ensure steady progress with consistent workflows.	Cam organized client training sessions during high-traffic hours and maintained fixed time slots for consultations. Ram developed a weekly calendar for assessments, check-ins, and client recovery tracking.
Focus on Time Management - Enhance productivity with efficient time use. - Avoid burnout by organizing the workday.	Cam streamlined daily operations by batching training sessions and reserving time for strategic planning. Ram blocked dedicated hours for deep work, including program research and performance analysis.
Develop Self-Discipline - Strengthen resolve by completing tasks even when motivation dips. - Create habits that sustain effort.	Ram worked through detailed financial reports and backend operations consistently. Cam maintained follow-ups with clients and leads daily, regardless of workload or distractions.
Prioritize Rest and Self-Care - Maintain mental and physical well-being for consistent performance. - Prevent burnout with self-care.	Ram implemented structured sleep hygiene and recovery protocols as part of his routine. Cam incorporated midday meditation and post-session runs to manage stress and restore energy.
Stay Focused on Your "Why" - Reinforce commitment by focusing	Cam cultivated long-term client relationships, turning the gym into a close-knit community. Ram

on the bigger picture. - Stay connected to your purpose.	continuously refined the Super Wellness Atelier's model to deliver transformative, data-driven results.
Celebrate Progress and Milestones - Boost morale through recognition. - Reinforce positive cycles of effort and reward.	Cam celebrated team wins with appreciation events and reward programs. Ram reinvested in innovative equipment and tools when their key performance goals were met.
Lead by Example - Inspire your team with consistent effort. - Foster a culture of dedication and productivity.	Cam's enthusiasm and reliability motivated clients and peers alike. Ram's commitment to evidence-based practice and innovation sets the standard for client success.

Key Takeaways:

- Success is built on consistent action, showing up daily, following structured routines, and adapting to challenges with discipline and focus.
- Whether through strategic planning or relentless execution, long-term results require sustained effort, time management, and resilience.
- Maximize individual strengths, complement team members' approaches, and stay aligned with your shared vision to create a lasting impact.

Self-Assessment: Are You Cultivating a Strong Work Ethic?

Rate yourself on each statement from 1 (Never) to 5 (Always):

1. I set clear, achievable goals that guide my daily work.
2. I follow a consistent schedule that prioritizes important tasks.
3. I use time management techniques to maximize productivity.
4. I practice self-discipline and push through challenging tasks.
5. I balance work with rest and prioritize self-care to avoid burnout.
6. I stay focused on my "why" to maintain motivation and resilience.
7. I celebrate small achievements to stay motivated and reinforce progress.
8. I lead by example, demonstrating a strong work ethic to others.

Score Interpretation:

- **35-40:** You are consistent, productive, and resilient.
- **25-34:** Improve focus and follow-through to boost results.
- **15-24:** Build discipline, time management, and goal-setting.
- **Below 15:** Prioritize structure to avoid burnout and inconsistency.

Author's Tip: Keep working and stay committed even when enthusiasm fades to get extraordinary results.

1.3.2. Networking and Relationship-Building

Entrepreneurial success is not what you know but who you know. A strong network opens doors to new opportunities, valuable resources, and game-changing insights to drive your growth and strengthen your resilience. Whether mentors and investors or peers and employees, the people you connect with become key to your business's success.

Take Mark Zuckerberg, for instance. Facebook began as a college project, but the support of early investors and advisors helped transform it to become a global giant. His story demonstrates that networking is about meeting the right people and forging relationships that drive your vision forward.

Building a strong network isn't a luxury; it's a necessity. Surrounding yourself with seasoned mentors can help you sidestep costly mistakes and make better choices. The right connections can introduce you to investors who share your vision, potential partners who complement your strengths, and customers who trust your brand. More than that, networking offers an emotional support system - because entrepreneurship is not supposed to be a solo journey.

A well-connected entrepreneur is also a trusted entrepreneur. Trust is not built overnight, but when you're part of a strong network, you become credible and build strong, synergetic relationships.

Without networking, entrepreneurs miss out on critical advice, funding opportunities, and collaborations that could have been pivotal to their success. The road becomes lonelier, growth slows, and opportunity doors remain closed.

In business, relationships aren't just helpful; they are the bridges to your next big opportunity. This segment will equip you with the tools to build a thriving network that supports your long-term goals and helps you turn connections into lasting success.

The Power of Networking in Super Wellness Atelier

Ram and Cam's thriving fitness business, Super Wellness Atelier, wouldn't be where it is today without their ability to build meaningful relationships. While Ram excelled at strategic networking with industry professionals, suppliers, and media outlets, Cam's charm and hands-on approach made him the go-to connection at fitness expos and community wellness events. Together, they transformed their networking efforts into a powerhouse of opportunities, partnerships, and business growth.

Let's explore how Ram & Cam demonstrated networking and relationship-building, and the lessons we can learn from their journey.

Steps & Key Focuses	Ram & Cam's implementation journey
Identify Key Individuals and Groups - Connect with individuals aligned with your aspirations. - Engage with relevant groups, networks, and communities.	Ram created a list of gym equipment suppliers, sports therapists, and fitness influencers who aligned with their brand vision. Cam joined local fitness meetups and wellness events to build organic connections.
Build a Value-First Approach - Create meaningful, mutually beneficial relationships. - Show genuine interest in others' goals.	Cam offered free training sessions to influencers and collaborated with wellness brands for joint events. Ram provided industry insights to equipment suppliers, strengthening their partnerships.
Follow Up and Stay Connected - Maintain long-term connections through consistent follow-ups. - Demonstrate authentic commitment.	Ram sent follow-up emails and thank-you notes within 24 hours of networking events, while Cam nurtured relationships by celebrating client milestones and engaging with collaborators regularly.
Leverage Social Media for Professional Networking - Increase visibility and maintain connections online.	Ram used LinkedIn and professional networks to connect with industry experts and share updates on their recovery techniques. Cam kept social media followers engaged with

- Participate actively in industry discussions.	behind-the-scenes content and interactive fitness challenges.
Develop Strong Communication Skills - Build trust through empathy and clarity. - Foster rapport with engaging and effective communication.	Ram's ability to ask thoughtful questions and actively listen built trust with investors and suppliers. Cam's storytelling and humour made clients feel part of the Super Wellness Atelier family.
Engage in Mentorship or Peer Groups - Foster collaboration and mutual growth. - Gain and share knowledge through shared experiences.	Ram joined a local entrepreneur mastermind group to exchange business insights. Cam participated in fitness coaching networks, brainstorming innovative training programs with other professionals.
Nurture Long-Term Relationships - Build trust and loyalty through meaningful, consistent interactions.	Ram kept in touch with suppliers and media contacts through regular updates and appreciation messages. Cam organized community workout events, fostering strong relationships with clients and wellness partners.

Key Takeaways:

- Success grows through who you know - build authentic connections, not just contacts.
- Network strategically to unlock new opportunities, resources, and collaborations.
- Nurture relationships with consistency, building trust and offering value first.

Self-Assessment: Are You Cultivating Networking and Relationship-Building Skills?

Rate yourself on each statement from 1 (Never) to 5 (Always):

1. I identify and connect with key individuals who can support my growth.
2. I network at events or industry conferences to meet new contacts.
3. I approach networking with a value-first mindset, looking to offer help and support.
4. I build relationships by keeping in touch.
5. I use social media platforms for professional networking.
6. I practice active listening and effective communication in networking.
7. I participate in mentorship groups and mastermind groups.
8. I maintain long-term relationships by staying connected and offering support.

Score Interpretation:

- **35-40:** You build strong relationships that unlock growth.
- **25-34:** Targeted improvements can boost your networking impact.
- **15-24:** Focus on follow-ups, adding value, and attending events.
- **Below 15:** At risk of isolation. Prioritize networking to avoid missed opportunities.

Author's Tip: Treat networking as an investment, not an afterthought. Build genuine relationships by offering value first, listening intently, and staying authentic.

1.3.3. Customer-Centric Mindset

Success in entrepreneurship isn't just about having a great product - it's about deeply empathizing with your customers and solving their problems meaningfully. A customer-centric mindset ensures that your business isn't just selling but truly serving, building trust and loyalty that fuel long-term growth.

Arlene Dickinson, a Canadian entrepreneur and former Dragon on Dragons' Den, built her marketing firm Venture Communications by profoundly understanding client needs and consumer behaviour. She didn't just sell marketing services; she helped brands connect authentically with their audiences. She earned long-term trust by putting customers at the center of every campaign and built a reputation for delivering real value.

When customers feel heard and valued, they don't just return - they become your biggest advocates, spreading the word and strengthening your reputation. A customer-first approach creates loyal buyers who drive repeat sales, spark organic referrals and boost profitability. More than that, businesses that focus on solving actual pain points become indispensable in their customers' lives. Positive experiences lead to glowing reviews and brand goodwill that no marketing budget can buy.

Businesses that don't listen risk losing their audience to competitors who do. Growth stalls, retention drops, and brand reputation suffer without taking customer feedback seriously. A business that doesn't prioritize its customers doesn't just struggle - it fades into irrelevance.

This segment will provide actionable strategies for developing a customer-centric mindset, helping you build genuine relationships with your audience and create solutions that keep them returning for more.

Building a Customer-Centric Business at Super Wellness Atelier

Ram and Cam knew that Super Wellness Atelier would only thrive if their clients felt valued and supported. While Ram focused on using data to track performance trends and refine services, Cam took a hands-on approach - engaging with clients in the gym and through social media to understand their needs firsthand. Together, their customer-first mindset became the foundation of their success.

Let's explore how Ram & Cam demonstrated a customer-centric mindset and the lessons we can learn from their journey.

Steps & Key Focuses	Ram & Cam's implementation journey
Listen to Customer Feedback Actively - Understand client needs and pain points. - Use feedback to drive meaningful improvements.	Cam gathered insights by chatting with clients post-workout and running Instagram polls, while Ram monitored reviews and fitness progress data to refine their training programs.
Map the Customer Journey - Create a seamless experience at every touchpoint. - Address pain points to improve customer satisfaction.	Ram designed a flowchart outlining every client interaction, from onboarding to progress tracking, identifying areas for improvement. Cam personalized training plans and sent encouraging messages to keep clients motivated.
Empathize with Client Needs and Pain Points - Make informed decisions based on genuine client feedback. - Prioritize solutions that address real challenges.	Cam tested alternative workout plans for clients struggling with injuries or mobility limitations, while Ram fine-tuned recovery protocols based on client data.
Focus on Customer Service Excellence - Build trust through responsive and effective service. - Strengthen loyalty with positive client interactions.	Cam trained staff to greet every client by name and ensure a welcoming atmosphere, while Ram streamlined the sign-up and scheduling process for a frictionless experience.
Gather and Use Data-Driven Insights - Align offerings with client	Ram tracked session attendance, workout preferences, and recovery progress to optimize fitness plans.

behaviour. - Use insights to tailor programs and marketing.	Cam analyzed social media engagement to spot trends and introduce new class formats.
Engage with Clients Regularly - Strengthen relationships through consistent communication. - Show appreciation for client engagement.	Cam ran fitness challenges and social media giveaways, while Ram sent personalized messages celebrating client milestones, like their first pull-up or a completed marathon.
Empower Your Team to Be Client-Centric - Foster a culture that prioritizes client satisfaction. - Recognize and reward customer-focused behaviors.	Ram led monthly training sessions to reinforce a client-first mindset, while Cam recognized team members who went above and beyond for clients with incentives and shout-outs.
Iterate and Improve Based on Feedback - Stay adaptable to evolving client expectations. - Use feedback to refine and enhance offerings.	Ram reviewed client feedback and performance data quarterly to adjust training methods. Cam encouraged clients to share suggestions and implemented changes to enhance their experience.

Key Takeaways:

- Listen actively and build genuine connections to create a customer-centric experience.
- Use empathy and data-driven insights to deliver services that meet real client needs.
- Engage regularly and adapt based on feedback to stay relevant, innovative, and client-focused.

Self-Assessment: Are You Cultivating a Customer-Centric Mindset?

Use this self-assessment to evaluate your current approach to building and maintaining a customer-centric mindset. Rate yourself on each statement from 1 (Never) to 5 (Always):

1. I actively listen to customer feedback.
2. I have mapped the customer journey to identify and improve each stage of the experience.
3. I empathize with my customers and understand their pain and needs.
4. I prioritize customer service excellence and resolve issues quickly and effectively.
5. I use data to gain insights into customer preferences and behaviour.
6. I engage regularly with customers to show them they are valued and heard.
7. I encourage a customer-centric mindset within my team, ensuring everyone focuses on customer needs.
8. I iterate and improve products or services based on customer feedback.

Score Interpretation:

- **35-40:** Highly customer-centric.
- **25-34:** Improve in key areas to better meet customer needs.
- **15-24:** Boost empathy, feedback use, and service to strengthen ties.
- **Below 15:** Urgent need to adopt a more customer-focused approach.

Author's Tip: Listen to customer feedback, anticipate future needs, and consistently exceed their expectations. Your customers aren't just buying your product but investing in your brand story.

1.3.4. Financial Acumen

Financial literacy is an essential trait for all successful entrepreneurs. When financing your business, financial acumen helps you to evaluate investor proposals, bargain for favourable terms, and make informed decisions about debt and equity. Also, strong financial skills help you take calculated risks that drive growth without depleting resources. Carefully planning your budget ensures you utilize your resources effectively, allowing you to achieve objectives without unnecessary excess. Knowing how to manage cash flow keeps your business running smoothly and prevents your well-thought-out plans from collapsing due to an avoidable cash crunch.

Without financial acumen, even the most promising businesses can run into trouble. Poor financial management can lead to cash shortages, stalling operations, and forcing difficult compromises. Mismanaged cash flow can turn a minor challenge into a significant crisis. Entrepreneurs who don't understand financial strategy risk being caught up in unfavourable financing agreements, hindering their ability to expand.

Financial acumen is also a vital life skill, in addition to being excellent for business. You will leave this session with practical strategies to help you become more financially informed, make better life decisions, and ensure your business stays on the path to long-term success.

Financial Acumen - The Backbone of Super Wellness Atelier's Success:

Ram and Cam's experience owning Super Wellness Atelier instilled them with the realization that financial acumen is equally as important as creative training practices and client engagement. While Cam brought energy and creativity to workouts and skills for marketing, Ram made certain that their fiscal infrastructure was robust and sustainable. They discovered the value of marrying their expansion plans with sensible financial management.

Let's see how Ram & Cam demonstrated financial acumen and the lessons we can take from their experience.

Steps & Key Focuses	Ram & Cam's implementation journey
Learn Basic Financial Concepts - Build foundational knowledge to make informed decisions. - Understand key metrics to track success.	Cam took the lead in learning financial basics to ensure the business had a solid foundation. Though more instinct-driven, Ram supported this by participating in financial discussions and gradually picking up concepts like profit margins and revenue forecasting.
Create and Manage a Budget - Align finances with business objectives. - Ensure resources are being utilized effectively.	Cam created and managed the budget, ensuring expenses aligned with business goals. He regularly reviewed costs and curbed Ram's occasional overspending on experimental recovery tools.
Track Cash Flow Regularly - Maintain liquidity to avoid cash shortages. - Prepare for fluctuations in revenue.	Cam monitored cash flow closely, identifying opportunities to save (e.g., bulk purchasing deals). Ram contributed by forecasting potential expenses tied to new innovations and growth ideas.
Set Financial Goals and Metrics - Align financial activities with strategic goals. - Use metrics to measure progress.	Cam set big-picture revenue targets and introduced the idea of using performance metrics. Ram implemented seasonal promotions and tailored offerings to drive revenue and meet financial targets.
Use Financial Tools and Software - Simplify financial management through automation.	Cam researched and introduced accounting software and tech integrations for client performance tracking. Ram used the data from

- Gain real-time insights into financial health.	these tools to make operational and pricing decisions.
Understand Funding Options - Choose funding strategies that align with your needs. - Evaluate risks and benefits carefully.	Cam researched small business grants and low-interest loans. Ram explored sponsorships and partnerships with wellness brands to gain additional funding and exposure.
Review Financial Statements Regularly - Gain a clear understanding of financial health. - Identify areas for improvement.	Cam scheduled monthly financial reviews, analyzing profit and loss statements and cash flow trends. He translated the numbers into actionable insights for Ram.
Seek Financial Advice When Needed - Avoid costly mistakes through expert guidance. - Optimize financial strategies for growth.	Cam engaged with an accountant for tax planning and financial structuring. Ram learned from these sessions and applied the guidance to reinvest in client experience and manage expansion.

Key Takeaways:

- Use financial discipline to guide decisions and ensure growth aligns with your resources.
- Balance creativity with thoughtful financial planning to build sustainable, long-term success.
- Track your financial health regularly to stay proactive and avoid costly mistakes.

Self-Assessment: Are You Cultivating Financial Acumen?

Rate yourself on each statement from 1 (Never) to 5 (Always):

1. I understand basic financial concepts like cash flow, profit margins, and budgeting.
2. I create and manage a budget for my business to track income and expenses.
3. I regularly monitor my cash flow to ensure sufficient working capital.
4. I set financial goals and use metrics to track performance.
5. I use financial tools to streamline financial management tasks.
6. I understand different funding options and their pros and cons.
7. I review financial statements regularly to stay informed about my business's financial health.
8. I seek financial advice from experts to make informed decisions.

Score Interpretation:

- **35-40:** Strong financial skills.
- **25-34:** Improving key areas will boost budget and cash flow control.
- **15-24:** Build knowledge in budgeting and financial basics.
- **Below 15:** Urgent need to develop financial management skills.

Author's Tip: Master the art of budgeting, cash flow management, and strategic financial planning to make every dollar work harder for your business, ensuring entrepreneurial success.

1.3.5. Long-Term Perspective

The goal of entrepreneurship is to create something that lasts, not just make quick money. A long-term perspective allows entrepreneurs to prioritize meaningful long-term impact over short-term gains, ensuring their companies grow sustainably and remain competitive.

Think of Google's founders, Larry Page and Sergey Brin. Instead of focusing on immediate financial gain, they made significant investments in research, development, and innovation. Because of the leadership's commitment to sustained expansion, Google has become a multinational behemoth that is still influencing and reshaping the world.

Thinking long-term means making decisions anchored to the vision with the help of operating principles, investing in enhancing adaptability and resilience, and, when necessary, re-inventing the business. Above all, a forward-thinking approach fosters the trust and loyalty of key stakeholders, investors, and consumers to stick with companies that demonstrate vision, consistency, and dependability.

Seeking quick cash can lead to missed opportunities for innovation, strained customer relationships, and a company that cannot change when the time comes because it is always in reactive mode instead of actively planning for the future.

A long-term perspective is a way of thinking, not just a plan. This segment will provide helpful insights on cultivating an optimistic outlook that propels long-term expansion, stimulates creativity, and positions your company for success.

Building a Long-Term Perspective:

Ram and Cam's experience with Super Wellness Atelier was a testament to the strength of a vision over the long haul. While Cam tended to get enamoured with ideas and quick victories, Ram grounded the company in sustainability, growth, and retention of clients. Together, they balanced innovation and long-term perspective, creating a brand that wasn't just successful but built to last.

Let's learn how Ram & Cam showed long-term thinking and what we can do from their experience.

Steps & Key Focuses	Ram & Cam's implementation journey
Define Your Core Purpose and Mission - Anchor decisions in purpose. - Create a meaningful foundation for growth.	Ram crafted a mission statement centred on delivering high-performance fitness training that promotes longevity and resilience. Cam ensured the brand messaging and client experience aligned with this mission.
Set Strategic, Sustainable Goals - Focus on steady, sustainable growth. - Align efforts with overarching objectives.	Ram broke their vision into five-year plans, prioritizing milestones like increasing client retention and expanding their service offerings. Cam contributed innovative marketing campaigns that drove short-term engagement while aligning with long-term growth.
Reinvest in Innovation and Development - Stay competitive through innovation. - Prioritize continuous improvement to meet client needs.	They allocated part of their budget to research and development, testing recovery-focused training programs, and integrating new fitness tech. Cam led weekly brainstorming sessions to generate fresh workout concepts.
Think Ahead to Market Trends and Changes - Anticipate market shifts to remain agile. - Adapt strategy proactively to meet evolving needs.	Ram researched the increasing demand for data-driven fitness and introduced wearable performance-tracking programs. Cam monitored social media trends to identify popular workout styles and adapt class offerings accordingly.
Measure Progress with Long-Term Metrics - Use data to make informed decisions.	Ram tracked key performance indicators (KPIs) like client retention rates, membership renewals, and profit margins. Cam celebrated milestones, such as

- Evaluate success based on long-term metrics.	reaching 500 successful client transformations.
Develop a Resilient Mindset - Strengthen persistence and adaptability. - Learn and refine strategies after challenges.	Ram saw challenges, like fluctuating membership rates, as opportunities to refine their business model. Cam embraced setbacks, using them to create adaptive solutions like launching virtual training programs during off-peak seasons.
Build a Culture of Continuous Learning - Keep the team prepared for long-term challenges. - Encourage skill-building and adaptability.	Ram hosted training sessions on client psychology, injury prevention, and business development. Cam recognized and rewarded team members who contributed innovative ideas to program development and customer engagement.

Key Takeaways:

- Prioritize sustainable growth to stay relevant, impactful, and thrive long-term.
- Balance innovation, customer focus, and resilience to build lasting success.
- Continuously reinvest, track progress, and strengthen client relationships to stay ahead.

Self-Assessment: Are You Cultivating a Long-Term Vision?

Rate yourself on each statement from 1 (Never) to 5 (Always):

1. I have a clear purpose and mission that goes beyond short-term profits.
2. I set sustainable, long-term goals that guide my business's growth.
3. I reinvest resources in innovation and development to maintain competitiveness.
4. I stay informed about industry trends and future market changes.
5. I use long-term metrics to track progress, such as customer retention and brand loyalty.
6. I prioritize building strong, lasting relationships with customers.
7. I view challenges as learning opportunities that contribute to long-term resilience.
8. I foster a culture of continuous learning and adaptation within my team.

Score Interpretation:

- **35-40**: You are positioned for sustainable growth and lasting impact.
- **25-34**: Strengthen key areas to improve strategic planning and sustainability.
- **15-24**: Prioritize purpose, reinvestment, and customer ties to build long-term impact.
- **Below 15**: Urgently work on your long-term.

Author's Tip: A long-term vision is your entrepreneurial compass. Following it will ensure your decisions today build a strong foundation for tomorrow's success.

Part 2 - Entrepreneur's Journey

Introduction: A Crash Course in Conquering the Business World

Welcome to the wild ride of entrepreneurship, where big dreams meet bigger challenges. This part is your survival guide, packed with wisdom, strategy, and just a sprinkle of humour to keep you sane while you chase your entrepreneurial destiny.

Whether you're nurturing a seed of an idea or scaling a business to new heights, the path of an entrepreneur requires resilience, adaptability, and a deep understanding of yourself and your venture. In this part of the book, we'll guide you through the essential stages of this journey, breaking it into three key sections to help you navigate your way effectively.

Section 2.1: Realizing the Dream

Every incredible journey begins with a compelling vision. This section will explore how to identify your purpose, articulate your big idea, and map out your entrepreneurial goals. You'll learn to harness your passion, build clarity, and set the foundation for future endeavours. From understanding your "why" to cultivating an innovative mindset, this is where your story begins.

Section 2.2: Where the Magic Happens - Operations

The entrepreneurial road is seldom smooth. This section focuses on every entrepreneur's hurdles and how to overcome them with grace and determination. You'll discover strategies for managing risks, handling uncertainty, and learning from failures. We'll also delve into the emotional and mental resilience needed to push forward, making this section your survival guide for the rocky terrains of entrepreneurship.

Section 2.3: Evolving and Closing the Journey

Once the foundation is in place and most obstacles have been successfully navigated, the focus shifts to growth and scalability. This section takes you through building strong systems, forging impactful connections, and scaling your business sustainably. You'll learn to cultivate leadership skills, manage teams effectively, and leverage opportunities to reach new horizons. It's about taking your entrepreneurial journey to its pinnacle.

Together, these three sections provide a roadmap for every aspiring entrepreneur, offering insights, tools, and inspiration to turn dreams into reality. With each segment, you'll uncover the skills and strategies needed to thrive at every stage of your journey, ensuring you succeed and excel in your chosen path.

So buckle up, dreamer! This part of the book isn't just a guide - it's your trusty co-pilot for navigating the twists and turns of building a business you'll be proud of. Let's make magic happen!

Section 2.1: Realizing the Dream

2.1.1. Where Dreams Begin - Ideation

From Idea to Impact: How Sandy Discovered the Power of Ideation

Sandy and Bay, long-time childhood buddies and former classmates, caught up over coffee after many years. As they chatted, Sandy enthusiastically talked about his latest endeavour - an innovative AI-powered app that lets clients design their shoes with complete customization.

"Imagine designing your dream shoes from scratch, selecting each characteristic, including colour, material, and even the sole type," Sandy grinned excitedly.

Bay listened carefully but sensed something missing in Sandy's story. She asked, "This is very innovative, but how much time did you spend on ideation before building the app?"

Sandy hesitated, caught off guard. "Well, I had the app idea, solved the technical feasibility, and jumped straight into development. Why?"

Bay smiled knowingly. "Sandy, it appears you skipped a critical step - ideation. It's the process of generating, exploring, and refining ideas. If you don't do it, you will miss out on determining the product market fit, as you have not systematically researched and recognized your target audience's needs, wants, and pain points."

Sandy looked intrigued. "So, what exactly is ideation?"

What Is Ideation and Why Is It Important?

Bay described ideation as implementing creative solutions to challenges or opportunities. It's not brainstorming; it's understanding the market, empathizing with your audience, assessing feasibility, and testing the validity of your ideas. Without ideation, your solution might not appeal to users or address their problems.

Here's why ideation matters:

1. **User-Centered Design:** You align your product and service with real customer needs.

2. **Innovation:** It helps you explore diverse and unconventional ideas.

3. **Problem-Solving:** You dig deeper into potential challenges and find solutions.

4. **Market Validation:** You test ideas before heavy investment, saving time and resources."

Sandy nodded. "I see what you mean. But how do I start ideating now?"

Applying Ideation: Sandy's Journey

Bay guided Sandy through the ideation process, breaking it into actionable steps. Together, they devised a plan to refine Sandy's AI-powered app idea. Below is how Sandy applied ideation.

Step	Actions and Outcomes
Understand Users	- Conducted online surveys targeting shoe enthusiasts, designers, and casual buyers. - Hosted focus groups with diverse participants to gather insights into their pain points and aspirations. **Outcome:** - Learned that users value personalization but often struggle with user-friendly interfaces. - Identified a demand for eco-friendly and ergonomic designs.
Define the Problem	- Synthesized feedback from surveys and focus groups to identify recurring themes. - Conducted competitive analysis of existing shoe customization apps. **Outcome:** - Realized the app lacked inclusivity for different foot shapes and sizes. - Found a gap in sustainable design options.
Brainstorm Ideas	- Organized a structured brainstorming session with his team, using methods like mind mapping and the "How Might We" technique*. - Explored unconventional ideas, even those initially deemed impractical.

	Outcome: - Generated ideas such as: 1. AI-powered foot measurement for precise fit. 2. Materials transparency showing the environmental impact of choices. 3. Collaborative design options for group projects or gifting.
Prototype Solutions	- Built clickable wireframes using available tools to visualize user flows. - Created a low-fidelity prototype focusing on the core features identified during brainstorming. **Outcome:** - Enabled users to test: 1. A virtual try-on feature using augmented reality. 2. Drag-and-drop customization for colours, patterns, and materials. 3. Accessibility features for visually impaired users.
Test and Refine	- Conducted usability tests with 20 beta testers representing different demographics. - Collected quantitative data (completion rates) and qualitative feedback (verbal comments and observations). **Outcome:** - Discovered that some features were overly complex, leading to confusion. - Simplified the interface based on feedback. - Built a "guided design" mode for first-time users.
Explore Market Fit	- Conducted a pre-launch campaign on social media to gauge interest and validate demand. - Partnered with a small group of eco-conscious influencers to spread the word. **Outcome:** - Gained over a hundred sign-ups for early access within a week.

	- Attracted potential B2B clients interested in branded designs for corporate gifts.
Iterate and Innovate	- Incorporated feedback into iterative prototypes and retested with new users. - Worked with sustainability experts to refine material sourcing. **Outcome:** - Created a polished product with robust features like eco-impact metrics and precision-fit designs. - Crafted a business opportunity with a strong Unique Selling Proposition (USP).

*"How Might We" technique is a design thinking method that reframes problems into questions to encourage creative problem-solving and innovation by focusing on opportunities rather than solutions.

In a subsequent meeting, Bay beamed, "See? By ideating, you've transformed a good idea into one that truly addresses customer needs." Sandy smiled, thankful for Bay's knowledge. "I guess this coffee session was worth more than all the caffeine in the world!" he joked. Together, they toasted creativity, innovation, and the power of ideation.

Key Takeaways:

- Think boldly - no idea is too big at the start.
- Validate your idea with honest feedback and deep market research.
- Refine continuously until your concept is ready to launch.

Self-Assessment: How Hot is Your Idea?

Answer the following questions on a scale of 1 (not at all) to 5 (absolutely). Add up your score to see how solid your idea is!

1. Does your idea solve a real problem for a specific group of people?
2. Have you done enough market research to understand your audience's needs?
3. Have you identified at least one competitor, and how your idea stands out?
4. Have you assessed whether your idea is feasible with your current resources?
5. Have you received constructive feedback from others?
6. Are you excited enough about your idea to work on it every day?
7. Can you explain your idea clearly in one sentence?

Score Analysis:

- **30-35**: Your idea is hot - time to get to work!
- **20-29**: It's solid, but do some fine-tuning.
- **Below 20**: Back to the drawing board, friend. It is okay - Einstein went through drafts, too.

Author's Tip: Great ideas are born where passion meets practicality. Keep your eyes open, your ears tuned, and your mind curious. Your "What if?" moment could be right around the corner.

2.1.2. Where Passion Meets Purpose - Planning

From Vision to Victory: How Omar Crafted a Roadmap to Success

Omar had always been passionate about photography, and after ideation, he concluded that he could turn his love for capturing moments into a business - a boutique photography service specializing in custom photo books and wall art. Excited but unsure how to proceed, Omar sought advice from his brother.

"You need to meet Trina," his brother said. "She's a business coach and can help you turn this passion into something real." Omar met Trina over coffee, eager to discuss his idea. After listening patiently, Trina leaned back and said, "Omar, you have a great idea, but an idea alone isn't enough. The next important step is creating a plan."

What is Planning, and Why is it Important?

Omar tilted his head. "What kind of plan? I want to take and sell photos, but isn't that enough?"

Trina smiled. "Not quite. Planning is about taking your passion and giving it structure and direction. This foundational work helps you figure out how to bring your idea to life, anticipate challenges, and stay focused on your goals."

Trina explained further Why Planning is Essential.

1. **Clarity:** A plan helps you break down your idea into actionable steps.
2. **Feasibility:** It tests whether your idea can work financially and operationally.
3. **Focus:** Planning keeps you aligned with your goals, preventing distractions.
4. **Risk Management:** It prepares you for potential challenges and shows you how to overcome them.
5. **Accountability:** A plan sets measurable milestones to track progress.

Omar was intrigued. "That makes sense. But where do I even start?" Trina outlined Omar's steps, breaking them into manageable tasks. Below is how Omar planned for his business.

Step	Actions and Outcomes
Define the Vision	- Clearly articulated the business idea: "A boutique photography service offering custom photo books and wall art." - Identified target customers: families, newlyweds, and small businesses seeking personalized photo products. - Created a vision statement: "To preserve life's precious moments through artistic and personalized photography solutions." **Outcome:** Defined the vision. Then, aligned the mission, purpose and operation principles with the Vision
Set Goals	- Defined **SMART** goals (Specific, Measurable, Achievable, Relevant, and Time-bound) objectives to ensure clarity and focus. - Set short-term goals: Launch the business within three months and complete five paid projects in the second quarter. - Set medium-term goals: Build an online store within 15 months and expand services to include photo restoration. **Outcome:** Established clear milestones to track progress and maintain momentum through the different growth phases.
Market Research	- Analyzed competitors offering similar services. - Conducted surveys to understand customer preferences and pricing expectations. - Researched trends in personalized photo products. - Discovered a demand for eco-friendly photo books. - Identified a pricing sweet spot for target customers.

	Outcome: Gained valuable insights to shape service offerings, pricing, and marketing strategies based on real customer needs and market trends.
Develop a Business Model	- Mapped out key revenue streams: photography services, custom photo books, and wall art. - Defined operational costs: equipment, marketing, and materials. - Considered potential partnerships with printing companies. - Finalized a business model that projected profitability within the first year. **Outcome:** Created a sustainable and flexible business structure designed to support profitability and scalability.
Create a Financial Plan	- Estimated start-up costs, including equipment upgrades and initial marketing campaigns. - Calculated break-even point and set pricing accordingly. - Secured initial funding through a small loan and personal savings. - Developed a budget for the first year of operations. **Outcome:** Planned for financial readiness and gained confidence in pricing to support a strong and stable business launch.
Outline Operations	- Determined workflows for photography sessions, editing, and product delivery. - Decided on turnaround times for custom projects. - Established a streamlined process to ensure timely delivery and maintain customer satisfaction. **Outcome:** Designed operational efficiency measures to ensure a smooth client experience and reliable service delivery.

Build a Marketing Plan	- Created a social media strategy to showcase portfolio and engage with potential customers. - Designed a website with a booking system and service details. - Launched social media pages with a consistent posting schedule. - Attracted first inquiries through social media. **Outcome:** Planned to establish brand presence and attract early interest, setting the foundation for ongoing customer engagement.
Plan for Growth	- Set up a feedback system to improve services based on customer reviews. - Identified opportunities for scaling: hiring assistants and expanding into corporate events. - Built a scalable plan for future growth while maintaining the boutique feel of the business. **Outcome:** Planned to position the business for sustainable growth while preserving its personalized approach.

Through Trina's guidance, Omar realized that turning passion into a business required more than enthusiasm. Following a structured planning process, Omar transformed his idea into a tangible plan that brought his vision to life and set him on a clear path to success. With a well-thought-out plan, Omar was ready to turn his passion into a thriving business.

Key Takeaways:

- Clarify your vision and set a clear, focused direction for your business.
- Identify risks and opportunities early to stay prepared and proactive.
- Stay organized, confident, and adaptable with a solid strategic plan.

Self-Assessment: Are You Planning Like a Pro?

Rate yourself on a scale of 1 (Not at all) to 5 (Absolutely) for each question below. Add up your score to see where you stand.

1. Do you have a clear and inspiring vision for your idea or business?
2. Have you set specific, measurable, and time-bound goals for your project or business?
3. Have you conducted thorough market research to understand your audience and competition?
4. Do you have a detailed business model outlining revenue streams, costs, and operations?
5. Have you created a financial plan, including budgeting and a break-even analysis?
6. Do you have a step-by-step operational plan to execute your idea?
7. Have you developed a marketing strategy to promote your business?
8. Do you regularly review and adapt your plan based on feedback and changing circumstances?

Score Analysis:

- **29-40:** You're a planning pro! Your strategy is solid and sets you up for success.
- **17-28:** You're on the right track, but there's room to refine your planning process.
- **8-16:** You're just starting - time to focus on building a strong plan.

Author's Tip: Passion sparks the idea and provides a purpose, but planning gives it structure and direction. Don't rush the process. Take time to map out your path because a well-crafted plan doesn't just move you forward; it keeps you focused when the road gets bumpy.

2.1.3. Show Me the Money! - Securing Financing

The Money Dance: "How Alena Mastered the Wisdom of Financial Fuel?"

Alena had always been fascinated by technology and its ability to solve everyday problems. While working full-time, she conceptualized an idea for an AI-powered home organization app that could declutter spaces virtually and offer personalized solutions. Her friends loved the idea, and after months of sketching designs and researching the market, Alena decided to turn her concept into a reality. She realized she had one big challenge during the planning process - money. Alena estimated that launching her app would require $120K, and her current savings wouldn't be enough. Determined, she set out to secure the financing she needed, one step at a time.

Why Securing Financing is Essential

Danny, a strategic business coach, shared this advice: "Alena, funding is the lifeblood of your business. Without it, even the most innovative ideas can stay trapped in your head. Securing financing isn't just about raising money; it's about backing your vision with the fuel it needs to take off." Danny explained why skipping financing could be detrimental:

- **No-Cash Crash**: Alena couldn't develop or market her app effectively without funds.
- **Missed Opportunities**: Lack of capital would prevent scaling and capturing market demand quickly.
- **Stress Overload**: Bootstrap or self-funding is not for everyone and every business. Limited resources could lead to a non-starter or provide subpar results depending on the investments required.

Alena and Danny worked together to create a financing plan. Here's how Alena approached financing.

Step	Actions and Outcomes
Assess Financing Needs	- Calculated start-up costs: app development, marketing, team hiring, and operational expenses, totalling $120K. - Identified specific expenditures: $65K for development, $20K for marketing, $20K for team, and $15K for operations. **Outcome:** Gained a clear, detailed picture of total capital requirements to move forward confidently.
Explore Funding Options	- Invested $60K of personal savings to show commitment. - Approached close friends and family, raising $30K. - Extended her personal Line Of Credit from $5K to $15K - Planned additional ways to fund the remaining gap, such as grants, partnerships, and side gigs. **Outcome:** Closed $105K of the $120K funding gap, built trust and demonstrated resourcefulness.
Build a Financial Plan	- Created a detailed breakdown of costs and timelines. - Designed a roadmap to stretch resources and focus on early Minimum Viable Product (MVP) launch. **Outcome:** Prioritized expected spending, enabling a lean MVP launch and setting a clear path for financial decision-making.
Leverage Personal Networks	- Reached out to friends and professional contacts to explore contributions like free design work or marketing advice. - Tapped into beta users from her network to test the app early. **Outcome:** Reduced expected early-stage costs and validated the product through real user insights.

Leverage Non-Monetary Support	- Joined start-up communities and accelerators for mentorship, tech support, and publicity. - Gained introductions to journalists, influencers, and beta testers, building credibility for the app. **Outcome:** Expanded visibility and support while strengthening credibility through third-party validation.
Stay Organized and Persistent	- Used financial tracking tools to monitor expenses. - Adjusted plans based on feedback from beta users and market response. - Maintained clear documentation of all financial decisions and progress milestones. **Outcome:** Controlled financials, stayed agile, and built a foundation for investor and stakeholder trust.

With financing secured, Alena launched the first version of her app within six months. A targeted marketing campaign attracted thousands of downloads in the first three months, and her user base continued to grow steadily. Alena turned her vision into a thriving start-up by staying focused on her goals and managing resources wisely.

Key Takeaways:

- Know your numbers, market, and value - prepare thoroughly to use every dollar wisely.
- Craft a clear financial plan that reflects both ambition and discipline.
- Be persistent and resourceful - sometimes support comes in ways other than money.

Self-Assessment: Are You Ready to Secure Funding?

Answer the following questions on a scale of 1 (not at all) to 5 (absolutely). Add up your score to see where you stand.

1. Have you identified the best financing option(s) for your business?
2. Do you understand the pros and cons of self-funding vs. external funding?
3. Have you created a professional, compelling pitch deck?
4. Can you clearly articulate your business idea and its market potential?
5. Have you practiced your pitch with mentors or trusted advisors?
6. Do you have early validation (e.g., customer interest, prototypes)?
7. Are you prepared to answer tough questions about your financial projections?

Score Analysis:

- **30-35:** Financially ready. Time to act!
- **20-29:** Solid foundation, but tighten up your plan.
- **Below 20:** Keep building - preparation is everything.

Author's Tip: Securing financing isn't just about the ask - it's about the story. Make your plan relatable and grounded in purpose, and people will want to support it in more ways than one.

2.1.4. Where Vision Takes Shape - Business Set-Up

How did Priya convert her Vision into a Venture?

Priya loved making candles; what began as a way to relax after work became a passion project when her friends couldn't stop raving about her unique scents and eco-friendly packaging. Encouraged by their enthusiasm, Priya turned her hobby into a full-fledged business: a sustainable candle brand.

However, Priya quickly realized that making candles and running a business were very different. With the help of her mentor, she embarked on the crucial journey of setting up her business appropriately.

Why Proper Business Setup Matters?

Priya's mentor explained: "Setting up your business is the bridge between your idea and reality. Skipping this step is like building a house without a foundation - it may look fine at first, but it won't last. A proper setup ensures legal compliance, operational efficiency, and a great customer first impression."

Risks of Skipping Business Setup:

- **Legal Issues:** Without proper registration, Priya risked running afoul of tax and regulatory authorities.

- **Operational Chaos:** Without systems, managing inventory, orders, and finances could become overwhelming.

- **Customer Dissatisfaction:** Unpolished products or services could lead to negative reviews and lost opportunities.

- **Stressful Fixes:** Delaying setup tasks could create bigger problems and extra costs later.

Here is how Priya set up her business.

Step	Actions and Outcomes
Select a Name and Register the Business	- Brainstormed and chose the name "Glowing Bright Candles." - Checked name availability, registered the business, and secured the domain. - Created a legally recognized brand identity. - Established credibility with customers and vendors. **Outcome:** Built a strong foundation and official presence for the brand.
Obtain Licenses and Permits and Complete Registrations.	- Applied for a business license and applicable permits – Registered for the local tax requirements with the Revenue Agency. - Purchased liability insurance to protect against unforeseen risks. - Ensured the product was as per Consumer Product Safety regulations under Health Authority regulations before scaling operations. **Outcome:** Became fully compliant and protected, enabling safe and legal business operations.
Set Up Financial Systems	- Opened a business bank account for transparency. - Set up accounting software to track sales, expenses, and taxes. - Simplified financial management and created budgets for raw materials, marketing, and packaging. **Outcome:** Gained financial control and clarity to support strategic decision-making.
Build Operational Workflows	- Created an inventory management system for wax, wicks, and packaging. - Used a scheduling tool to track production and order fulfillment.

	- Streamlined operations, reducing waste and ensuring timely delivery of orders. **Outcome:** Built an efficient and scalable operation that ensured product availability and customer satisfaction.
Develop Product Offerings	- Designed and tested three candle prototypes. - Gathered feedback from friends and family to refine scents, packaging, and pricing. - Launched three signature candles that were eco-friendly, beautifully packaged, and competitively priced. **Outcome:** Created a market-ready product line with strong appeal and a clear value proposition.
Establish Digital Presence	- Built a professional website with e-commerce functionality. - Created social media accounts to showcase products and share behind-the-scenes content. - Attracted hundreds of followers in the first month and secured pre-orders before the official launch. **Outcome:** Built online visibility and early customer traction before launch.
Secure Legal Protections	- Drafted clear terms and conditions for online sales. - Used contracts for wholesale orders with local retailers. - Purchased business insurance. - Protected the business from legal risks and established trust with partners and customers. **Outcome:** Established a legally protected and trustworthy business environment.
Soft Launch	- Hosted a small launch event with friends, family, and local influencers at her home. - Offered exclusive discounts to attendees. - Collected valuable feedback, built buzz on social media, and achieved her sales target before the official website launch.

	Outcome: Validated the product in a real market setting and generated momentum for the official launch.

Over time, Priya's candles have been sold in local boutiques and online. Her meticulous setup allowed her to focus on growth without being bogged down by operational headaches. Her customers raved about her products, and her sustainable practices resonated with her audience, helping her build a loyal customer base.

Key Takeaways:

- Stay legally compliant by registering your business and securing permits to avoid future risks.
- Set up strong systems for operations, finances, and inventory to run efficiently from the start.
- Invest in professionalism and testing to build trust and deliver a standout customer experience on day one.

Self-Assessment: Is Your Business Ready to Roll?

Answer the following questions on a scale of 1 (not at all) to 5 (absolutely). Add up your score to see if your setup is solid.

1. Have you officially registered your business with the appropriate authorities?
2. Do you have the necessary licenses, permits, and insurance in place?
3. Have you set up an efficient system for managing administrative tasks (e.g., banking, accounting, taxes)?
4. Have you prepared a physical or digital workspace that supports your business operations?
5. Have you finalized your product or service offering, ensuring it's customer-ready?
6. Have you tested your product or service and incorporated feedback?
7. Do you have a clear plan for managing daily operations?

Score Analysis:

- **30-35**: You're operationally bulletproof - go crush it!
- **20-29**: Good start, but shore up those weak spots.
- **Below 20**: You've got work to do, but Rome wasn't built in a day.

Author's Tip: Treat setup like assembling furniture - read the instructions (carefully), don't skip steps, and remember: the effort you put in now saves you major headaches later.

2.1.5. Showtime - Launch

How Sammy Mastered the Power of a Flawless Launch?

Sammy stood in a bustling public laundry facility, holding a bottle of FreshFlow, their newly developed eco-friendly laundry product. It was the culmination of months of hard work - formulating, testing, and refining a product designed to eliminate odour and stubborn stains while being gentle on fabrics and the planet. With a vision to revolutionize how people approach freshness in their laundry and homes, Sammy knew the launch was their chance to make a splash.

Time to Shine:

The launch phase is your business's moment in the spotlight. Sammy understood that this was more than just introducing a product; it was about creating a memorable experience, building trust, and setting the stage for long-term success: his strategy combined preparation, creativity, and a personal touch to connect with the target audience.

Why Skipping the Launch Plan Could Have Been a Disaster?

Sammy's cousin, who mentored him, warned about the risks of an unprepared launch:

- **The Ghost Town Effect:** A lack of buzz could result in zero sales or interest.
- **Missed Connections:** Without targeting the right audience, even the best product could flop.
- **Unpolished First Impressions:** Launching without thorough testing could lead to dissatisfied customers.
- **No Feedback, No Growth:** Missing insights from early users would mean losing opportunities to improve.

Sammy took this to heart and carefully planned out all aspects of every launch. Given below is how Sammy launched his firm.

Step	Actions and Outcomes
Create a Go-to-Market Strategy	- Defined the target audience: eco-conscious households, laundry business owners, and gym-goers. - Designed a marketing plan leveraging social media, partnerships, and local events. - Identified clear channels to reach customers and built anticipation for the product. **Outcome:** Established a strategic plan to enter the market with clarity and confidence.
Develop and Test Your Offering	- Distributed samples to a pilot group of 50 testers, including busy families and gym members, to gather feedback. - Adjusted the formula to enhance odour removal on athletic wear. - Refined the product based on real-world insights, ensuring effectiveness and customer satisfaction. **Outcome:** Created a proven, high-performing product tailored to real customer needs.
Build Pre-Launch Buzz	- Posted teasers featuring the product's eco-friendly ingredients and benefits on social media platforms. - Partnered with influencers specializing in sustainability to showcase the product. - Generated online excitement and attracted pre-orders from environmentally conscious shoppers. **Outcome:** Built a strong anticipation and demand for the product before launch.
Execute the Grand Launch	- Hosted a launch event at a local laundry facility with live demonstrations and free samples. - Offered discounts and freebies to attendees who made purchases during the event. - Created a buzz-worthy experience that resulted in immediate sales and enthusiastic word-of-mouth referrals.

	Outcome: Achieved a successful, high-energy launch that drove immediate engagement and conversions.
Monitor Performance and Gather Feedback	- Used web-based analytical service to track website traffic and sales. - Collected feedback from early customers via surveys and social media comments. - Gained insights into customer preferences, such as demand for larger bottle sizes and refill options. **Outcome:** Acquired actionable insights to optimize the product and customer experience.
Follow Up and Maintain Momentum	- Sent personalized thank-you emails with discount codes for future purchases. - Launched a social media campaign featuring customer testimonials and laundry tips. - Built strong relationships with early adopters and maintained interest with engaging content and promotions. **Outcome:** Strengthened brand loyalty and sustained interest through meaningful post-launch engagement.

Sammy's careful planning and creative approach paid off. Within the first month, FreshFlow sold hundreds of bottles, gained glowing reviews online, and attracted inquiries from local stores interested in stocking the product. Sammy successfully positioned FreshFlow Solutions as a go-to brand for eco-friendly freshness by combining a strong digital presence with an engaging launch event.

Key Takeaways:

- Define your target audience and craft a focused marketing plan before launch.
- Start with a pilot launch to gather feedback and fine-tune your product.
- Create buzz through social media, influencers, and events to build excitement and visibility.

Self-Assessment: Are You Ready for Showtime?

Answer the following questions on a scale of 1 (not at all) to 5 (absolutely). Add up your score to see how launch-ready you are.

1. Do you have a clear go-to-market strategy that outlines your audience, channels, and goals?
2. Have you built anticipation for your launch through teasers, promotions, or previews?
3. Have you tested your product or service with a smaller audience (pilot launch)?
4. Are you ready to adapt based on customer feedback?
5. Is your branding consistent and strong across all launch channels?
6. Do you have a plan for handling customer inquiries and potential issues post-launch?
7. Are you confident in your ability to make a memorable first impression?

Score Analysis:

- **30-35**: You're launch-ready. It is your time to shine!
- **20-29**: You're close, but refine your strategy to ensure success.
- **Below 20**: Take a deep breath, revisit your plan, and prep like a pro.

Author's Tip: Treat your launch like a party - plan, invite the right guests, and make sure everyone leaves talking about it. A successful launch isn't just about selling - it's about creating an unforgettable experience.

Section 2.2: Where the Magic Happens - Operations
Case Study: From Chaos to Clarity: Running the Company

The Overwhelmed Founder

Kai stared at the coffee cup before him, barely noticing the hum of the busy café around him. Across the table sat Susan, his business advisor, her notebook open and pen poised like a sword, ready to slash through his problems. Novalution Edge, Kai's tech start-up, had done what few could - developed a custom software product and a SaaS (Software as a Service) platform. The team's innovative genius was undeniable. The chaos in running the business? Equally undeniable.

"I don't know where to start," Kai admitted, running his hand through hair that had seen better days. "There's so much happening at once - product development, customer issues, trying to make sales - it's overwhelming."

Susan smiled, the calm anchor to Kai's storm. "We're going to take this step by step. First, tell me about your product operations. How are you managing development and delivery?"

Kai sighed so deeply that nearby customers turned to look. "Our custom software is great, but the development cycle is… messy. Deadlines are slipping, the team is burnt out, and we're constantly putting out fires instead of working strategically."

Taming the Operations Monster

Susan leaned in, her voice calm but firm. "Kai, operations is where the magic really happens. It's not just about writing brilliant code; it's about creating systems to ensure the magic is repeatable.

Kai squinted. "So, how do I fix it?"

"Start simple," Susan advised. "Document your development process - write down the steps from ideation to delivery like a roadmap. Establish clear workflows. Assign responsibilities so no one is confused about who does what. Set realistic timelines -

realistic being the keyword. Build in time for testing and feedback. Think of it like baking. You wouldn't pull a half-baked cake out of the oven, would you?"

Kai chuckled, finally showing signs of life. "Alright. Document, workflow, timelines, testing. Got it! But what about the SaaS platform? It's so different; it's running live while we still improve it."

The SaaS Beast: Automate or Die

Susan nodded. "True. SaaS isn't just about features; it's about reliability. Running it like a pro means uptime, seamless onboarding, and personal customer support."

Kai raised an eyebrow. "Seamless onboarding? How do I do that?"

"Automation," Susan declared with the conviction of a tech evangelist. "Set up automated user onboarding emails and create a robust knowledge base so customers can solve their problems quickly. For support, get a helpdesk system in place. And for uptime - monitor everything. Downtime isn't just a technical glitch; it's a trust killer."

Kai scribbled furiously. "Automate and organize. Got it! But let's talk about money. Keeping this whole thing afloat feels like juggling flaming torches blindfolded."

Facing the Financial Fog

Susan chuckled. "Ah, the financial nightmare. Here's the good news: it doesn't have to be a nightmare if you shine a light on it. Budgeting, tracking, and forecasting are your three weapons against financial chaos."

Kai groaned. "I'm not great with numbers."

"Then find someone who is," Susan said bluntly. "Hire a financial expert who can track your cash flow, create a budget that covers costs and expected revenue, and most importantly, forecast ahead. *What's your runway? What happens if a client pays late?* Knowing these numbers gives you control - and peace of mind."

Kai's brow furrowed. "Runway. Cash flow. Hire an expert. Got it! But Susan, I need more than control. I need sales."

Sales and Marketing: The Dynamic Duo

"Marketing and sales are two sides of the same coin," Susan explained. "First, define your ideal customer - for both the custom software and the SaaS. Then, create a strategy to reach them. Start simple: blogs, webinars, and partnerships to show your expertise. Use social proof - testimonials, reviews, and case studies. Trust is everything. Remember, sales isn't about pushing a product but demonstrating value and building relationships."

Kai leaned back, processing. "Demonstrating value and building relationships. Got it! And my current customers? How do I keep them happy?"

Keeping the Love Alive

Susan smiled knowingly. "Ah, the forgotten art of keeping the love alive. Happy customers are your best marketers. Proactively check in with them. Listen to their feedback. Solve their problems before they become complaints. A loyal customer is worth their weight in gold - they'll tell everyone about you without you asking them to do so."

Kai exhaled deeply as though the weight of the world had just been lifted from his shoulders. For the first time that day, he smiled. "Okay, Susan, this feels doable now. Systems, automation, finances, team, sales, and customers. I've got a plan."

Susan raised her coffee cup in a mock toast. "One step at a time, Kai. Novalution Edge is your dream, and together, we'll make it unstoppable."

As Kai walked out of the café, his steps were lighter, and his mind clearer. He didn't yet have all the answers, but he finally had a plan - and that was a start.

2.2.1. Running a Business - Like a Pro

Running a company can often feel like juggling flaming swords on a unicycle. For Kai, founder of Novalution Edge, the chaos was very real. With a custom software product and a live SaaS platform, Kai's team was brilliant at building technology but struggled to bring order to the madness of deadlines, customer issues, and sales. Enter Susan, his business advisor, who helped Kai transform from an overwhelmed founder to a "PRO" business operator.

What did Kai do? Here is how Kai accomplished 'Running a Business Like a Pro.'

Steps	Actions and Detailed Outcomes
Document Development Processes	- Mapped out each phase of the software development cycle (e.g., ideation, development, testing, deployment) - Defined team roles and responsibilities - Created a shared repository for documentation. **Outcome:** Clear workflows, improved accountability, and reduced bottlenecks.
Set Realistic Timelines	- Broke projects into smaller, manageable milestones. - Used project management tools to assign and track tasks. - Incorporated buffer time for unexpected delays. **Outcome:** Projects were delivered on time, reducing stress for the team.
Implement Agile Methodology	- Conducted daily stand-up meetings for updates and issue resolution. - Used sprints (short, time-boxed periods where a team works to complete a set amount of work) to prioritize and deliver incremental progress. - Gathered feedback at the end of each sprint.

	Outcome: Flexible adaptation to changes and improved team collaboration.
Streamline SaaS Operations	- Automated user onboarding with welcome emails, tutorials, and guides. - Established a monitoring system to ensure uptime and performance. - Regularly updated and tested SaaS features. **Outcome:** Enhanced user experience and reduced operational errors.
Set Up Quality Assurance (QA)	- Created testing protocols for custom software and SaaS platforms. - Used automated testing tools where applicable. - Scheduled regular manual tests to check usability. **Outcome:** High-quality, bug-free products and services that meet customer expectations.
Establish Feedback Loops	- Regularly collected feedback from team members about processes. - Used customer feedback to refine operations. - Implemented a feedback system that encourages continuous improvement. **Outcome:** Processes that evolve and improve based on real-world input.
Monitor Key Metrics	- Tracked metrics such as development velocity, customer churn rate (the percentage of customers who stop doing business over a specific period), and uptime percentage. - Used dashboards to visualize and analyze data. - Adjusted operations based on trends and findings. **Outcome:** Data-driven decision-making and proactive problem resolution.

Align Team with Company Goals	- Communicated long-term objectives and how each role contributes to them. - Hosted regular alignment meetings to discuss progress and challenges. - Recognized and rewarded achievements tied to company goals. **Outcome:** A motivated and aligned team drives the business forward.
Build Scalable Systems	- Identified repetitive tasks and automated them. - Choose tools and software that grow with the company. - Documented scalable workflows to handle increasing demand. **Outcome:** Operations that adapt seamlessly to growth without additional strain.

Key Takeaway:

- Document processes and implement scalable systems for efficient, high-quality delivery.
- Prioritize automation to boost efficiency and support growth.
- Use feedback and data to improve and align operations with business goals on an ongoing basis.

Self-Assessment: Are You Running Your Business Like a Pro?

Answer the following questions on a scale of 1 (not at all) to 5 (absolutely). Add up your score to see where you stand.

1. Have you documented your core business processes?

2. Do you set realistic timelines and consistently deliver on schedule?

3. Are you using structured methodologies (like Agile) to manage work, adapt to changes, and keep your team aligned?

4. Have you automated operations to improve efficiency?

5. Is there a consistent quality assurance process in place to ensure your product or service meets high standards?

6. Do you regularly track and analyze key metrics (KPIs) to make informed, data-driven decisions?

7. Is your team aligned with your company's long-term goals and motivated to contribute to its success?

Score Analysis:

- **30-35**: You're running your business like a pro! Systems are solid and scalable.

- **20-29**: You're close! Tighten up processes and keep refining your operations.

- **Below 20**: Time to hit pause and work on building the systems that will help you scale and succeed.

Author's Tip: Great businesses are built with happy clients and effective team members. Your operations are the bridge between the two, so prioritize them. Regularly review and update workflows and processes to eliminate inefficiencies and adapt to changes in technology or market demands. Like Kai, stay proactive.

2.2.2. Keeping Your Business in the Black (and Your Sanity Intact)

When Kai first sat across from Susan with a coffee cup and a frazzled look, finances were the last thing he wanted to discuss. Numbers gave him nightmares, and cash flow felt like an unsolvable mystery. But Susan knew that to turn Novalution Edge into a thriving, resilient business. Kai needed to master the art of "Keeping Your Business in the Black - and Your Sanity Intact."

Through strategic steps and practical actions, Kai tackled his finances step by step, turning uncertainty into confidence and chaos into clarity.

Here is how Kai accomplished 'Keeping the Business in the Black.'

Steps	Actions and Detailed Outcomes
Create a Budget	- Listed all fixed and variable expenses (e.g., salaries, tools, utilities). - Estimated expected revenues from both the custom software and SaaS products. - Allocated funds for unforeseen expenses. **Outcome:** A clear financial roadmap guided spending and ensured adequate resource allocation.
Track Expenses	- Implemented accounting software to record every transaction. - Categorized expenses into operational, marketing, and development costs. - Conducted regular reviews to identify trends and eliminate unnecessary spending. **Outcome:** Real-time visibility into spending reduced waste and improved efficiency.
Monitor Cash Flow	- Created a cash flow statement to track money in and out. - Ensured sufficient cash reserves for a minimum of 3 months of operations.

	- Addressed gaps between receivables (the money customers owe for goods or services they have received but not yet paid for) and payables (the amounts the company owes to its suppliers for goods and services purchased) by optimizing invoicing cycles. **Outcome:** Sustained liquidity and operational stability without disruptions.
Forecast Revenue	- Analyzed past performance and the current sales pipeline. - Used industry benchmarks to predict growth and refine revenue targets. - Adjusted forecasts regularly based on market conditions and sales progress. **Outcome:** Data-backed revenue projections helped guide strategic decisions and set realistic goals.
Manage Invoicing and Payments	- Automated invoicing with clear payment terms. - Followed up promptly on overdue invoices. - Used tools to monitor accounts receivable and payable for a steady cash flow. **Outcome:** Timely payments improved client relationships and reduced cash flow delays.
Optimize Pricing Strategy	- Conducted market research to understand competitors' pricing. - Evaluated the value delivered to customers and adjusted prices. - Introduced tiered pricing for SaaS to attract different customer segments. **Outcome:** Competitive pricing ensured profitability while expanding market reach.

Monitor Financial Metrics	- Tracked key metrics: gross margin, net profit margin, and operating expenses. - Used financial dashboards to visualize KPIs for better insights. - Conducted monthly reviews to ensure financial goals remained on track. **Outcome:** Insightful metrics revealed risks and opportunities, enabling proactive decisions.
Prepare for Taxes	- Hired a tax consultant to ensure compliance and leverage deductions. - Maintained detailed records of all expenses. - Set aside funds monthly to cover tax liabilities. **Outcome:** Smooth tax filing process with no last-minute surprises or penalties.
Build an Emergency Fund	- Set aside a percentage of monthly profits for emergencies. - Invested in liquid assets to ensure quick accessibility. - Reserved the fund strictly for critical needs. **Outcome:** Financial resilience to weather unexpected downturns or challenges.

Key Takeaways:

- Track budgets and cash flow to eliminate overspending and maintain financial control.
- Use revenue forecasting and innovative pricing to drive sustainable profitability.
- Monitor financial metrics, prepare for taxes, and build reserves for long-term stability.

Self-Assessment: Keeping the Business in the Black?

Answer the following questions on a scale of 1 (not at all) to 5 (absolutely). Add up your score to see where you stand.

1. Have you created (and regularly updated) a clear budget that tracks expected revenues and all expenses?
2. Do you actively monitor your cash flow to ensure you have enough reserves to cover 3-6 months of operations?
3. Are your invoicing and payment processes streamlined, with timely follow-ups on overdue invoices?
4. Have you developed realistic revenue forecasts based on past performance, market trends, and your current sales pipeline?
5. Is your pricing strategy optimized to balance profitability, market competitiveness, and customer value?
6. When making decisions, do you consider key financial metrics like profit margins, operating expenses, and cash reserves?
7. Have you set aside funds for taxes and emergencies to avoid surprises and maintain financial stability?

Score Analysis:

- **30-35**: You're financially savvy!
- **20-29**: You're on the right path but must fine-tune a few areas.
- **Below 20**: Revisit your financial strategy, track your numbers, and seek expert advice to regain control.

Author's Tip: Treat your finances like your business's health. Regular check-ups (cash flow reviews), good habits (tracking expenses), and periodic professional consultations will keep your business in great shape!

2.2.3. Building Your Dream Team

When Kai first launched Novalution Edge, he dreamed of building an innovative, unstoppable company.

However, his firm's growth couldn't be attained without filling the gaps in personnel. He was doing too many things - CEO, coder, salesman, and office administrator - and it could not continue. That's when his advisor, Susan, helped him understand a hard truth: the strength of a business depends on its people.

Kai needed a dream team to grow Novalution Edge. A team with strengths supporting Kai's weaknesses. A team that shared the same vision. With Susan's guidance, Kai developed an organized and step-by-step process to form his dream team.

Here is how Kai built his dream team.

Steps	Actions and Detailed Outcomes
Define Roles and Responsibilities	- Introduced clear and specific job descriptions for every role. - Associated job responsibilities with business goals to encourage and ensure focus. - Introduced measurable key performance indicators (KPIs) for all job roles. **Outcome:** Improved accountability and productivity as team members understood their roles and expectations.
Hire for Skills and Culture Fit	- Developed a structured hiring process, including role-specific criteria. - Used interviews and assessments to evaluate technical skills, communication, and adaptability. - Prioritized candidates who aligned with Novalution Edge's values of innovation and collaboration. **Outcome:** A cohesive, well-rounded team that enhanced efficiency and fostered a positive work environment.

Invest in Onboarding	- Designed a comprehensive onboarding program with welcome resources, tools, and mentors. - Set short-term goals to help new hires integrate quickly and feel successful early on. - Assigned a buddy system (a procedure in which two individuals, the "buddies," operate together as a single unit so that they can monitor and help each other) for team support. **Outcome:** Faster adjustment, higher engagement, and reduced turnover rates among new hires.
Offer Training and Development	- Organized workshops and role-specific skill enhancement sessions. - Provided access to online courses and learning platforms for continuous education. - Encouraged cross-functional training to promote collaboration and versatility. **Outcome:** A skilled, confident workforce capable of adapting to evolving challenges and responsibilities.
Foster Open Communication	- Scheduled regular team meetings, one-on-ones, and company-wide updates. - Introduced a team communication platform tool to streamline communication among remote and onsite teams. - Actively encouraged feedback and addressed concerns promptly. **Outcome:** Improved trust, collaboration, and team morale across the company.
Build a Recognition Program	- Created a recognition system to reward outstanding performance with bonuses, awards, and public appreciation.

	- Celebrated milestones and team successes with team lunches or events.
	- Encouraged peer recognition through dedicated platforms and boards.
	Outcome: Motivated employees who felt valued and appreciated, driving higher engagement and performance.
Develop Career Growth Plans	- Identified individual growth opportunities for team members based on strengths and aspirations.
	- Designed personalized career roadmaps with actionable milestones.
	Outcome: Increased employee retention as team members saw long-term career potential within the company.
Establish Clear Policies	- Developed an employee handbook outlining expectations, policies, benefits, and conflict resolution procedures.
	- Introduced policies for remote work, flexible hours, and time-off requests.
	- Ensured policies were easily accessible and well-communicated.
	Outcome: A structured, transparent work environment minimized confusion and supported team harmony.
Conduct Performance Reviews	- Implemented regular performance cycles with a mix of self-assessment, peer feedback, and manager input.
	- Provided constructive feedback to help team members grow and succeed.
	- Set clear, actionable goals for improvement and recognition of achievements.
	Outcome: Improved staff performance alignment with company objectives.

Encourage Team Bonding	- Organized team-building activities, fun and interactive events, offsite retreats, and volunteer days.
	- Created informal opportunities for team interaction, like lunch-and-learns.
	- Celebrated diversity and inclusivity with cultural events and celebrations.
	Outcome: Stronger team cohesion, increased collaboration, and a supportive workplace culture.

Key Takeaways:

- Define clear roles and responsibilities to boost accountability and empower strengths.

- Hire for both skills and cultural fit to build a collaborative, high-performing team.

- Invest in training, communication, and recognition to foster loyalty, trust, and sustained growth.

Self-Assessment: Are You Building Your Dream Team?

Answer the following questions on a scale of 1 (not at all) to 5 (absolutely). Add up your score to see where you stand.

1. Have you clearly defined roles and responsibilities for every position on your team with measurable KPIs?
2. Do you have a structured hiring process that ensures candidates are a strong fit for both skills and company culture?
3. Have you implemented a comprehensive onboarding process to help new team members integrate quickly and effectively?
4. Do you invest in your team's development and career growth?
5. Is there open, consistent communication within your team, supported by tools and regular check-ins?
6. Do you have a system to recognize and reward good performance?
7. Have you created clear policies and procedures that promote fairness, transparency, and a positive team culture?

Score Analysis:

- **30-35**: You're building a dream team!
- **20-29**: Focus on refining your hiring, development, and recognition strategies.
- **Below 20**: Revisit your roles, processes, and people strategies to build a stronger foundation.

Author's Tip: Good leaders create strong teams. Invest time, energy, and care into your hiring process and culture development. Conduct regular one-on-one meetings to understand individual challenges, align goals, and nurture trust. A strong team isn't just good for business - it makes the journey much more fun.

2.2.4. Light the Path to Your Brilliance! - Marketing

Kai, the founder of Novalution Edge, ensured the world knew about his great products. After transforming his operations and building his dream team, Kai faced his next challenge: *how to market Novalution Edge effectively*. With Susan's guidance, he realized that great businesses don't just happen - they shine because their value is clear, their story is compelling, and their audience feels understood.

Susan helped Kai craft a marketing strategy that positioned Novalution Edge as a standout solution in a competitive market. Here is how Kai accomplished 'Lighting the Path to Brilliance.'

Steps	Actions and Detailed Outcomes
Identify Target Audience	- Defined ideal customer personas for both the custom software and SaaS platform. - Segmented the audience by demographics, behaviours, and pain points. - Conducted market research to validate the target segments and understand their needs. **Outcome:** A clear audience understanding enabled focused and highly effective marketing strategies.
Develop a Value Proposition	- Highlighted the unique benefits of both the custom software and SaaS offerings. - Tailored messaging to address specific customer pain points. - Ensured consistent messaging across the website, social media, and sales channels. **Outcome:** Strong, compelling communication that resonated with potential customers and differentiated Novalution Edge from competitors.
Create a Marketing Plan	- Set clear short-term and long-term marketing goals aligned with business growth. - Allocated a realistic budget for campaigns, tools, and resources.

	- Planned campaigns across multiple channels, including social media, email, and paid ads. **Outcome:** A structured roadmap ensured marketing efforts were efficient, goal-oriented, and impactful.
Build a Website and Online Presence	- Designed a professional, user-friendly website optimized for search engines (SEO). - Included detailed product descriptions, case studies, customer testimonials, and a blog. - Established engaging social media profiles on platforms where the target audience was most active. **Outcome:** Created enhanced online visibility and credibility, driving higher website traffic and engagement.
Leverage Content Marketing	- Created blogs, eBooks, and case studies to educate and inform the audience. - Developed video tutorials and webinars to showcase expertise and solutions. - Used storytelling to build emotional connections with potential customers. **Outcome:** Established authority, increased audience engagement, and attracted inbound leads through valuable content.
Implement Email Marketing	- Built a segmented email list for targeted communication. - Created automated email campaigns for users' onboarding, promotions, and updates. - Used A/B testing* to optimize subject lines, content, and send times. **Outcome:** Strengthened relationships with existing and potential customers, leading to improved conversion rates and loyalty.
Run Paid Advertising Campaigns	- Used online ads and social media ads to reach specific audience segments. - Retargeted website visitors and users who abandoned onboarding or carts. - Monitored ad performance and optimized campaigns for maximum return on investment (ROI).

	Outcome: Boosted brand awareness, generated leads, and delivered measurable results through targeted advertising.
Leverage Social Media	- Posted consistent, engaging content tailored to each platform's audience. - Used interactive social media features like polls, Q&A sessions, and videos to increase engagement. - Collaborated with influencers and industry leaders to expand reach. **Outcome:** Built a strong community presence, increased brand recognition, and engaged a loyal audience.
Monitor Marketing Metrics	- Tracked key metrics like website traffic, conversion rates, and customer acquisition costs. - Used analytics tools to identify trends and areas for improvement. - Adjusted marketing strategies based on data insights to optimize performance. **Outcome:** Data-driven decision-making led to continuous improvement and better return on marketing investments.
Engage in Partnerships and Networking	- Collaborated with complementary businesses for co-marketing opportunities. - Attended industry webinars, events, and meetups to build valuable connections. - Sponsored relevant events to gain visibility within targeted industries. **Outcome:** Resulted in expanded reach, credibility, and brand awareness through strategic partnerships and collaborations.

Key Takeaways:

- Know your audience and craft a compelling value proposition that solves their problems.
- Use a multi-channel strategy - content, social media, email, and ads - to maximize visibility and engagement.
- Track performance, optimize continuously, and build strategic partnerships to expand reach and credibility.

Self-Assessment: Are You Lighting the Path to Your Brilliance?

Answer the following questions on a scale of 1 (not at all) to 5 (absolutely). Add up your score to see where you stand.

1. Have you identified and segmented your ideal target audience?
2. Do you have a compelling value proposition communicating how your product or service solves your customer's problems?
3. Have you developed and implemented a structured marketing plan with clear goals, budget allocation, and chosen marketing channels?
4. Is your website professional, user-friendly, and optimized for search engines, showcasing your expertise and building trust?
5. Are you consistently creating valuable content (blogs, videos, case studies) that educates, engages, and attracts your target audience?
6. Do you actively use email marketing and social media to nurture relationships, build community, and drive engagement?
7. Are you tracking key marketing metrics and adjusting your strategies based on data to improve results continually?

Score Analysis:

- **30-35**: You're shining bright, positioning you as a leader.
- **20-29**: Refine your message for better reach and engagement.
- **Below 20**: Focus on understanding your audience and crafting a strategy for better performance.

*A/B Testing - You show one group of target audience version A (maybe a headline, button colour, or email subject line) and version B to another target audience group. Then you see which version people respond to better.

Author's Tip: Marketing is a marathon, not a sprint. Continuously test and optimize marketing campaigns through A/B testing to identify what resonates best with your audience. Stay consistent, experiment with new ideas and messages, and always put your customers at the center of everything you do.

2.2.5. Get Out There and Shine! - Sales

With Novalution Edge operating smoothly and his dream team in place, Kai focused on the next big challenge - sales. After all, even the best products need champions to get them into customers' hands. Susan reminded Kai of a simple truth: *a great business doesn't just solve problems; it connects with the right people and closes deals.*

Together, they built a robust, systematic sales process, allowing Novalution Edge to shine. Here's how Kai transformed his sales approach to take the company to the next level.

Here is how Kai accomplished 'Get Out There and Shine.'

Steps	Actions and Detailed Outcomes
Define Sales Goals	- Aligned sales goals with the company's overall business objectives. - Set clear revenue and customer acquisition targets. - Broke down goals into monthly, quarterly, and annual benchmarks. **Outcome:** Focused, measurable targets directed the sales team's efforts and enabled progress tracking.
Build a Sales Pipeline	- Identified the sales process stages, including lead generation, qualification, proposal, and closing. - Used a CRM (Customer Relationship Management) system to track and manage leads efficiently. - Continuously refined the pipeline based on results and feedback. **Outcome:** A structured pipeline ensured prospects moved smoothly through the sales journey.
Develop a Lead	- Leveraged content marketing, social media, and paid ads to attract potential leads.

Generation Strategy	- Implemented referral programs to encourage word-of-mouth leads. **Outcome:** A steady flow of high-quality leads entered the pipeline, fueling consistent growth.
Qualify Leads	- Established clear criteria to assess each lead's fit and readiness to buy. - Conducted discovery calls and surveys to gather relevant information. - Focused efforts on high-potential prospects to maximize conversion rates. **Outcome:** Efficient allocation of resources to leads most likely to convert, saving time and effort.
Customize Sales Pitches	- Tailored sales presentations to address each prospect's unique challenges and needs. - Highlighted the distinct benefits of both the custom software and SaaS platform. - Used case studies, client testimonials, and success stories to build credibility. **Outcome:** Personalized pitches increased engagement and boosted close rates.
Build Relationships with Prospects	- Followed up consistently using emails, calls, and in-person meetings. - Shared valuable insights, industry resources, and updates to provide ongoing value. - Took time to understand prospects' challenges and offer tailored solutions. **Outcome:** Stronger connections that led to trust, loyalty, and long-term partnerships.

Master Objection Handling	- Anticipated common objections, such as pricing, timing, and features concerns. - Prepared thoughtful responses that addressed concerns and demonstrated value. - Practiced active listening to understand objections empathetically. **Outcome:** Kai turned hesitations into commitments, improving the team's ability to conduct effective sales meetings.
Close Deals Effectively	- Used clear and concise language during negotiations to avoid confusion. - Provided transparent pricing, terms, and options to build trust. - Created urgency with limited-time offers and incentives to encourage prompt decisions. **Outcome:** Faster deal closures with minimal friction, driving revenue growth efficiently.
Upsell and Cross-Sell	- Identified opportunities to offer additional products, features, or upgrades that added value. - Introduced tiered plans and bundled packages to meet diverse needs. - Regularly reviewed customer accounts for potential upsell opportunities. **Outcome:** Resulted in increased revenue per customer while enhancing satisfaction and loyalty.
Monitor Sales Performance	- Tracked key performance metrics such as close rates, sales cycle length, and average deal size. - Conducted regular performance reviews with the sales team to identify gaps and opportunities.

| | - Adjusted strategies based on data insights and customer feedback. |
| | **Outcome:** Continuous improvement ensured alignment with sales goals and sustained success. |

Key Takeaways:

- Set clear goals and build a structured pipeline to focus efforts and drive consistent conversions.
- Customize pitches, qualify leads, and handle objections to boost connection and close rates.
- Track performance, upsell, and cross-sell to maximize revenue and continuously improve results.

Self-Assessment: Are You Ready to Get Out There and Shine?

Answer the following questions on a scale of 1 (not at all) to 5 (absolutely). Add up your score to see where you stand.

1. Have you set clear sales goals and broken them into achievable monthly or quarterly targets?
2. Do you have a structured sales pipeline that moves prospects smoothly from lead generation to closing?
3. Do you consistently generate high-quality leads through content marketing, networking, or referrals?
4. Do you have a process for qualifying leads so that you can focus on those most likely to convert?
5. Are your sales pitches customized to address each prospect's unique needs, backed by case studies or success stories?
6. Do you proactively handle objections and turn hesitations into commitments with empathy and confidence?
7. Are you tracking key sales metrics (like close rates or sales cycle length) and continuously using data to improve your process?

Score Analysis:

- **30-35**: Your sales process is strategic and streamlined
- **20-29**: Fine-tune your sales approach and strengthen key areas.
- **Below 20**: Adhering to an effective sales process will help connect, enhance closing rates, and grow faster.

Author's Tip: Develop a comprehensive sales playbook with strategies, scripts, objection-handling techniques, and case studies. Consistency is key to scaling success.

2.2.6. Keeping the Love Alive! - Customer Service

After refining operations, building a dream team, and perfecting the sales process, Kai realized one crucial truth: *acquiring customers is only the beginning.* To create a lasting business, Novalution Edge should nurture client relationships, ensuring loyalty and enhancing the customer's lifetime value.

Susan, ever the guiding force, told Kai, *"Great companies don't just serve customers; they make customers feel valued and understood."* Together, they developed a strategy to turn clients into lifelong advocates.

Here is how Kai accomplished 'Keeping the Love Alive.'

Steps	Actions and Detailed Outcomes
Understand Customer Needs	- Conducted surveys and interviews to gather insights. - Analyzed customer behaviour, feedback, and support tickets to identify pain points. - Prioritized solutions based on key customer challenges and desired outcomes. - Closed the loop by informing customers about changes made based on their feedback. **Outcome:** A deep understanding of customer expectations allowed Kai to offer tailored solutions that resonated with customers. Customers felt valued and heard, leading to increased loyalty and stronger relationships.
Streamline Onboarding	- Designed a clear, step-by-step guide for new users. - Provided a guided setup process with personalized onboarding sessions. - Implemented regular check-ins during the first 30 days to address challenges. **Outcome:** Faster adoption and a positive initial experience led to reduced churn and happier clients.

Provide Excellent Customer Support	- Set up a responsive helpdesk with multiple contact channels (email, chat, phone). - Developed a comprehensive self-service knowledge base with FAQs, guides, and videos. - Trained the support team to resolve issues effectively. **Outcome:** Quick issue resolution improved satisfaction, trust, and overall customer experience.
Foster Ongoing Engagement	- Sent regular email newsletters with updates, product tips, and success stories. - Invited customers to webinars, product showcases, and Q&A sessions. - Built an online community forum where users could connect, share experiences, and exchange ideas. **Outcome:** Stronger relationships, increased engagement, and a sense of belonging among customers.
Offer Personalized Experiences	- Leveraged data to tailor communications, product recommendations, and feature suggestions. - Offered customized pricing and add-ons for key accounts. - Rewarded loyal customers with exclusive perks, discounts, or personalized thank-you messages. **Outcome:** Personalized interactions strengthened connections and enhanced customer value.
Proactively Address Issues	- Monitored customer accounts for signs of dissatisfaction, such as reduced usage or negative feedback. - Proactively reached out to resolve potential problems before they escalated. - Created a dedicated team to handle high-risk accounts and restore trust. **Outcome:** Prevented churn, built trust, and reassured customers of Novalution Edge's commitment to excellence.

Recognize and Reward Loyalty	- Developed a loyalty program that offered rewards, discounts, and referral bonuses. - Highlighted success stories and loyal customers through case studies or public recognition. - Sent personalized messages or gifts during milestones like anniversaries or birthdays. **Outcome:** Strengthened long-term relationships and turned loyal customers into vocal advocates.
Provide Regular Updates	- Shared regular updates about product enhancements, new features, and upcoming releases. - Kept customers informed during service changes or scheduled downtimes. - Maintained transparency with timely communication. **Outcome:** Kai reinforced customer trust and confidence in Novalution Edge's reliability and innovation.
Measure Customer Success	- Defined and tracked key metrics such as retention rates. - Conducted quarterly customer satisfaction reviews. - Used insights to continually refine strategies for improving the customer experience. **Outcome:** Data-driven improvements resulted in stronger satisfaction, loyalty, and long-term success.

Key Takeaways:

- Proactively meet customer needs with tailored solutions, seamless onboarding, and outstanding support.

- Engage continuously through feedback loops and reward loyalty to turn customers into advocates.

- Deliver regular updates and measurable improvements to keep customers at the center of your strategy.

Self-Assessment: Are You Keeping the Love Alive?

Answer the following questions on a scale of 1 (not at all) to 5 (absolutely). Add up your score to see where you stand..

1. Do you truly understand your customers' needs through regular feedback, surveys, or direct conversations?

2. Is your customer onboarding process informative, supportive, and designed to ensure early success?

3. Do you provide responsive, empathetic, and effective customer support across multiple channels?

4. Are you consistently engaging your customers through newsletters, webinars, or community spaces?

5. Do you collect and act on customer feedback - and let them know when changes are made based on their input?

6. Do you personalize the customer experience with tailored communications, offers, or rewards?

7. Have you implemented strategies to recognize and reward loyal customers, turning them into advocates?

Score Analysis:

- **30-35**: Your clients likely feel valued, supported, and loyal.
- **20-29**: Focus on deepening engagement with more personal touches.
- **Below 20**: Start listening to your customers more and show them they truly matter!

Author's Tip: Implement a system to gauge customer satisfaction regularly. Use the feedback to uncover opportunities for improving experiences and increasing loyalty.

Section 2.3: Evolving and Closing the Journey

2.3.1. Getting It Done and Making It Count - Deliverables

How Sarah Transformed Deliverables into Growth for Her Eco-Friendly Skincare Brand?

Sarah always believed in creating skincare that was gentle on the planet and nourishing for the skin. Her eco-friendly skincare brand, NatureGlow, had a loyal following of customers who appreciated her commitment to sustainability and quality. However, as her business grew, Sarah faced challenges meeting customer expectations during the crucial delivery phase. Delays, plain packaging, and a lack of post-purchase engagement led to missed opportunities for repeat business and referrals.

Determined to address these challenges, Sarah shifted her focus to refining her deliverables, seeing them not as the end of the sales process but as an opportunity to build loyalty and drive revenue. Sarah transformed her business by reimagining the delivery process as a moment to delight customers and strengthen her brand.

Why Deliverables Are Essential for Success?

Sarah could hear her business coach's voice in her head explaining why deliverables were more than just logistics:

- **Build Trust:** Reliable and timely delivery creates confidence in your brand.
- **Encourage Loyalty:** Memorable experiences turn one-time buyers into repeat customers.
- **Gather Insights:** The delivery process is an opportunity to collect valuable feedback for continuous improvement.
- **Boost Revenue:** Happy customers result in fewer returns, more referrals, and increased lifetime value.

With this advice in mind, Sarah set out to make NatureGlow's deliverables a cornerstone of her customer experience.

Here is how Sarah excelled in providing deliverables for NatureGlow.

Step	Actions and Detailed Outcomes
Plan Product Delivery	- Collaborated with a green logistics partner for secure, sustainable shipping. - Rolled out biodegradable, high-end packaging that complemented the brand's green values. - Refreshed website FAQs and included explicit shipping timelines to manage customer expectations. **Outcome:** Customers had a seamless, authentic experience and appreciated the brand's values reflected in the unboxing.
Ensure a Seamless Experience	- Introduced quality checks to ensure all products were up to standard before shipping. - Included handwritten thank-you notes and product samples with orders. - Automated email notification to remind customers of the status of their order. **Outcome**: Enhanced customer satisfaction with a human touch and pre-emptive communication to make each delivery memorable. - Rolled out a subscription service for skincare staples, delivering convenience and value.
Gather and Act on Feedback	- QR codes are inserted within packages to facilitate feedback surveys, and the respondents are rewarded with discounts. - Responded to feedback by optimizing packaging design and bundling packages. **Outcome:** Gained actionable insights that enabled Sarah to improve the delivery experience and offerings regularly.

Build Revenue Streams	- Introduced bundle packs and initiated a referral program to drive bigger buys and new customer acquisition. **Outcome**: Sarah promoted repeat buying and customer loyalty, generating consistent revenue growth.
Build Long-Term Relationships	- Followed up with personalized thank-you notes, usage tips, and special offers through emails. - Implemented a VIP loyalty program with benefits such as early sales access and special samples. **Outcome**: Encouraged customer loyalty and a feeling of exclusivity, promoting long-term connections and word-of-mouth recommendations.
Train the Team for Excellence	- Established Standards for packaging and shipping procedures to maintain consistency. - Trained personnel in resolving customer issues promptly and empowered them with tools for effective service. **Outcome:** Provided consistent, high-quality service with a team equipped to handle challenges effectively.
Leverage Technology for Efficiency	- Used appropriate apps to automate order management and inventory monitoring. - Applied analytics to track delivery times, errors, and retention rates. **Outcome:** Improved efficiency in operations, decreased errors, and enhanced the effectiveness of the delivery process.
Monitor and Improve Performance	- Conducted monthly audits of delivery metrics and customer feedback. - Introduced express shipping options to accommodate the growing demand for faster delivery. **Outcome**: Retained high delivery standards and aligned processes to evolving customer expectations.

Foster Customer Advocacy	- Encouraged customers to leave reviews and unboxing experiences by rewarding social media tags with discounts. - Featured leading advocates on social media, building a community of active customers. **Outcome:** Converted happy customers into vocal brand ambassadors, organically increasing NatureGlow's visibility.
Celebrate and Innovate	- Released seasonal gift sets and marked milestones with giveaways. - Added new product lines in response to customer demand and feedback. **Outcome:** Maintained the brand ethos, attracting new customers while delighting existing ones.

Sarah's new delivery process changed NatureGlow's customer experience in six months and drove growth.

Her customer loyalty increased, as did her revenue.

Sarah's success shows how focusing on deliverables can create loyal customers, drive word-of-mouth marketing, and strengthen a brand's reputation.

Key Takeaways:

- Deliver reliably and transparently, adding personal touches that reflect your brand values.
- Use customer feedback to refine processes and drive growth through subscriptions, bundles, and referrals.
- Build loyalty by following up, offering exclusive perks, and rewarding customer advocacy.

Self-Assessment: Are You Crushing Your Deliverables?

Answer the following questions on a scale of 1 (not at all) to 5 (absolutely). Add up your score to see where you stand..

1. Do you deliver your product or service on time and in excellent condition?
2. Are your delivery methods aligned with your brand values (e.g., eco-friendly, fast)?
3. Do you communicate delivery expectations clearly to customers?
4. Are you actively collecting feedback from your customers after delivery?
5. Do you use customer feedback to make meaningful improvements?
6. Do you have systems in place to encourage repeat purchases or subscriptions?
7. Are you maximizing revenue opportunities through upselling or referral programs?

Score Analysis:

- **30-35**: Your deliverables are spot on - your customers must love you!
- **20-29**: You're doing well, but tightening up a few areas could boost your results.
- **Below 20**: Time to revisit your delivery game plan. Take baby steps and build from there.

Author's Tip: The delivery (value transfer) doesn't end when the product reaches the customer or when they receive the service. Follow up, gather feedback, and find ways to surprise and delight your customers. That's how you turn a transaction into a lasting relationship.

2.3.2. Doing Well by Doing Good - Social Responsibility

How Raj Made Social Responsibility the Heart of EcoShell?

Raj, the founder of EcoShell, always dreamed of creating more than just a product-based company. His bamboo-based reusable food wraps and utensils were already popular among eco-conscious consumers, but Raj wanted EcoShell to be known for its impact on the planet. He envisioned a business where every product sold contributed to sustainability on a global scale.

Motivated by this vision, Raj integrated Corporate Social Responsibility (CSR) into the core of EcoShell's operations. He turned CSR into a brand value and a business strategy by planting trees for every sale and raising awareness about sustainability.

Why Social Responsibility Matters for Business?

Raj's business advisor emphasized that incorporating social responsibility into business can have several benefits:

- **Build Trust:** Customers prefer brands that not only care about their profits, but also the community.

- **Inspire Loyalty:** Customers and employees support brands that share the same values as them.

- **Strengthen Identity:** CSR aligns a business with its mission, creating a memorable and relatable brand.

- **Make a Difference:** Businesses have the resources and platforms to create positive societal and environmental change.

Using this advice, Raj was able to come up with an authentic and impactful CSR strategy that perfectly aligned with his company's mission.

Step	Actions and Detailed Outcomes
Choose a Cause That Aligns With Your Brand	- Sustainability and reforestation were selected as core causes. - Pledged to plant a tree for every $500 revenue earned by the company. - Committed 10% of profits to sustainability education in schools. **Outcome:** EcoShell built a strong reputation as a brand dedicated to environmental impact, resonating deeply with eco-conscious customers.
Create an Actionable Plan	- Set measurable goals: plant 300 trees in the first year. - Partnered with non-profits for reforestation projects. - Allocated resources for both operational and philanthropic goals. **Outcome:** Achieved clear milestones, keeping the mission focused and transparent to stakeholders.
Involve Customers	- Allowed customers to choose reforestation projects at checkout. - Shared impact updates, including the number of trees planted. - Engaged customers through challenges with prizes for eco-friendly practices. **Outcome:** Turned customers into active participants in the mission, strengthening loyalty and advocacy.
Measure and Share Impact	- Tracked CSR metrics through detailed reports, such as trees planted in which locations. - Shared updates via infographics, videos, and social media posts. **Outcome:** Built customers' trust by showcasing tangible results, enhancing transparency and credibility.
Involve Your Team	- Organized team volunteer days, like park cleanups. - Encouraged staff to pitch CSR ideas during monthly

	meetings. - Highlighted employee contributions on the website and social media. **Outcome:** Fostered a mission-driven workplace culture, boosting employee engagement and morale.
Integrate CSR Into Marketing	- Featured impact stories on EcoShell's website and social channels. - Collaborated with influencers and eco-conscious bloggers to amplify the message. - Highlighted customer contributions to CSR milestones. **Outcome:** Raj increased brand visibility and authenticity, driving new customer interest and retention.
Foster Partnerships	- Partnered with schools to fund sustainability education programs. - Collaborated with other eco-friendly brands to co-host events like Earth Day giveaways. **Outcome:** Expanded EcoShell's reach and impact through mutually beneficial collaborations.
Celebrate and Share Milestones	- Hosted virtual events to celebrate milestones, like planting 100 trees. - Offered discounts and sneak peeks of new products during milestone celebrations. **Outcome:** Strengthened customer relationships and reinforced EcoShell's commitment to its mission.
Establish Governance and Oversight	- Appointed a CSR lead responsible for strategy execution, reporting, and partner vetting. - Allocated a dedicated CSR budget for ongoing and emergent initiatives. **Outcome:** Ensured long-term accountability, alignment with strategic objectives, and risk-managed CSR execution.

Within a year, Raj's CSR strategy transformed EcoShell into a locally known brand in the eco-conscious space. EcoShell's customers returned repeatedly, increasing revenue and reducing customer acquisition costs. By aligning its mission with its operations, EcoShell became a brand that customers loved, employees championed, and competitors admired.

Key Takeaways:

- Align social responsibility efforts with your brand and set clear, measurable goals.
- Engage customers and employees to build loyalty and a shared sense of purpose.
- Share impact transparently and continuously innovate to keep initiatives relevant and effective.

Self-Assessment: Are You a Socially Responsible Business?

Answer the following questions on a scale of 1 (not at all) to 5 (absolutely). Add up your score to see where you stand..

1. Have you identified a cause or initiative that aligns with your brand and values?
2. Do you have a clear plan for implementing and managing your CSR activities?
3. Are your customers aware of your CSR efforts and encouraged to participate?
4. Do you involve your team in CSR activities to build engagement and pride?
5. Are you measuring the impact of your CSR initiatives?
6. Are you communicating your CSR efforts transparently to stakeholders and customers?
7. Is your CSR strategy contributing positively to your brand reputation and business goals?

Score Analysis:

- **30-35**: You're a CSR superstar - keep making a difference!
- **20-29**: You're on the right track, but there's room to expand your efforts.
- **Below 20**: It's time to incorporate CSR into your business. Start small and grow your impact.

Author's Tip: Authenticity matters. Choose a cause that genuinely resonates with you and your team. Customers can tell when a business is doing CSR just for show, so make it meaningful and let your passion shine through.

2.3.3. Bring in the Big Guns - Investor Timing

How Elena Perfected Investor Timing for Soleil?

Elena, the founder of Soleil, was determined to revolutionize sustainable home solutions with her solar roof tiles. While her ideas were ground-breaking, she quickly realized that even the most innovative products require strategic funding to succeed. Instead of rushing to secure significant investments, Elena crafted a plan to match funding sources with her business's growth milestones, ensuring that every dollar raised aligned with her vision and needs.

Her plan had three key phases: prototype development, scaling up manufacturing, and expanding nationally. Elena could grow Soleil without compromising her mission or control by attracting the right funding at the right time.

Why Investor Timing Matters?

Elena's business advisor stressed the importance of timing in bringing in investors:

- **Optimize Valuation:** Raising funds at the right stage ensures a higher valuation and minimizes equity dilution.
- **Align Goals:** Matching the type of investor to the growth phase ensures resources and expertise align with business needs.
- **Harness Growth:** The availability of finance and resources at the right time allows businesses to seize market opportunities.
- **Build Partnerships:** Selecting investors who share your values creates long-term partners who champion your mission.

Having learned this, Elena strategically approached each funding round of financing, raising capital while retaining control over her company.

Below is how Elena managed Soleil's investor timing.

Step	Actions and Detailed Outcomes
Understand Your Funding Needs	- Mapped out financial milestones: $50K for prototype development, $200K to launch Soleil, $2M for scaling production, and $5M for national expansion. - Aligned funding needs with specific business objectives. **Outcome:** Created a clear financial roadmap that guided

	her funding strategy and ensured resources aligned with goals.
Self-Fund or Seek Friends-and-Family Support	- Used $30K from personal savings and secured $20K from supportive family members. - Focused on building a prototype and validating market demand without external interference. **Outcome:** Elena retained full ownership during the early stages while establishing product viability.
Pre-External Investment Assessment	- Conducted a deep dive into the business model's scalability, market size, and capital intensity. - Evaluated team's readiness for external investment, including alignment with long-term vision and appetite for dilution. **Outcome:** Gained clarity on which investor types best aligned with the business mission and stage.
Know Who and When to Approach for Seed Investments	- Pursued Angel investors who were passionate about sustainability. - Approached angel investors after securing pre-orders and validating demand. - Prepared flawless pitches, detailed financial projections, and a business plan that addressed key questions. **Outcome:** Raised $200K to launch Soleil and successfully create momentum for future funding rounds.
Prepare for Venture Capital Investment	- Refined the business model and financial projections to demonstrate scalability. - Collected sales data, gathered customer testimonials, and created an investor-ready pitch deck. - Researched VC firms that aligned with Soleil's mission and ethos. **Outcome:** Secured $2M in venture capital and used it to expand manufacturing, build a marketing team, and open a distribution center.

Time Late-Stage Funding	- Prepared meticulously for a $5M funding round for national expansion. - Highlighted profitability, market leadership, and plans for global reach to attract investors. **Outcome:** Secured funding to enter new markets, partner with major retailers, and strengthen Soleil's position as a leader in sustainable home solutions.
Be Strategic About Timing	- Timed funding rounds to align with milestones, ensuring higher valuations and minimal equity dilution. - Used metrics like revenue growth and customer retention to justify valuation increases. **Outcome:** Elena retained 60% ownership while scaling Soleil sustainably.
Maintain Relationships with Investors	- Provided regular updates, shared successes, and involved investors in key decisions. - Organized networking events to build trust and strengthen partnerships. **Outcome:** She turned investors into long-term allies, fostering collaboration and advocacy for Soleil.

Through strategic funding, Elena turned **Soleil** into a leader in sustainable home solutions. By aligning her funding strategy with her growth stages and values, Elena scaled her business and built a supportive network of investors who championed her mission.

Key Takeaways:

- Align funding needs with business milestones and growth stages for focused investment.

- Choose investors who share your vision and bring strategic value to your business.

- Be investor-ready with compelling pitches, solid financials, and a plan to build lasting partnerships.

Pros and cons of the various sources of funding:

Funding Source	Pros	Cons
Venture Capital (VC)	- Large funding potential - Access to mentorship and networks - No repayment is required if the business fails	- Loss of equity and control - High expectations for rapid growth - Time-consuming and competitive process
Angel Investors	- Flexible investment terms - Often experienced mentors - No monthly repayments	- Loss of partial ownership - Might have strong opinions on business direction - Hard to find the right investor
Bank Loans	- No loss of ownership - Structured repayment schedule - Good for stable businesses with predictable revenue	- Interest payments add financial pressure - Requires strong credit and collateral - Risk of default and asset loss
Crowdfunding	- Market validation before product launch - No equity loss in most cases - Engages early adopters and builds a community	- Requires strong marketing effort - Uncertain success; campaigns may fail - Funds might not be enough for growth
Bootstrapping (Self-Funding)	- Full control over the business - No debt or equity loss - Forces efficient spending	- High personal financial risk - Growth may be slow due to limited funds - Hard to scale without external funds

Government Grants & Programs	- Free money, no repayment required - Encourages innovation and small businesses - Provides credibility and legitimacy	- Competitive and lengthy application process - Restrictions on fund usage - Funding amounts may be limited
Revenue-Based Financing	- No loss of equity - Payments scale with business performance	- Repayments tied to revenue, reducing cash flow flexibility - Often higher costs than traditional loans
Corporate Partnerships / Strategic Investors	- Access to resources, distribution, and industry expertise - Potential for acquisition or long-term collaboration	- May involve exclusivity agreements or restrictions - A strategic investor may prioritize their interests over yours
Revenue from Early Customers (Pre-Sales & Subscriptions)	- Immediate cash flow without giving up equity - Validates product and service demand	- Requires a strong sales and marketing strategy - Might not be enough for large-scale growth

Self-Assessment: Are You Timing Your Investor Approach Correctly?

Answer the following questions on a scale of 1 (not at all) to 5 (absolutely). Add up your score to see where you stand.

1. Do you understand which type of investor aligns with your current business stage?
2. Can you clearly articulate your funding needs and how the money will be used?
3. Have you developed a solid business plan to attract early-stage investors?
4. Are you tracking your business performance to pitch confidently to VCs for scaling?
5. Do you have a clear exit strategy to present to late-stage investors or buyers?
6. Are you prepared to negotiate equity and terms that align with your goals?
7. Do you have a backup plan if your preferred funding source falls through?

Score Analysis:

*   **30-35**: You have a strong hold on investor timing.
*   **20-29**: Refine your strategy to align better with your goals.
*   **Below 20**: Start by matching your funding needs with the investor.

Author's Tip: Bring in investors when your business hits key milestones, not before. The right timing means better valuations, less equity dilution, and partners who align with your vision.

2.3.4. The Grand Finale - Exit

How did Keondra transition GreenNest from business to legacy?

Keondra, the founder of GreenNest, built her eco-friendly home solutions company from the ground up. Her journey started with a mission to create sustainable, stylish home decor that made eco-conscious living accessible and beautiful. Over ten years, GreenNest grew from a local favourite to a market leader, with a reputation for innovative products and an unwavering commitment to sustainability.

When it was time to move on, Keondra strategically planned her exit rather than marking it an end. She used this chance to reinforce the company's legacy. She watched GreenNest flourish and succeed solely because she started early and planned carefully.

Why a Thoughtful Exit Matters?

Keondra had learned the importance of an intentional exit strategy at a business expo.

- **Reap the Rewards:** An effective exit unlocks the financial value of years of hard work.
- **Preserve Legacy:** Smoothly transitioning ensures the business maintains its mission and vision.
- **Foster Stability:** Planning the handover thoroughly ensures there's no impact on employees, customers, and operations.
- **Create New Opportunities:** A smooth exit can result in financial freedom to pursue personal goals or new ventures.

Keeping this in mind, Keondra prepared for the exit precisely and purposefully. Here's how she did so:

Step	Actions and Detailed Outcomes
Plan Your Exit Strategy Early	- Set clear goals: achieve a targeted valuation and secure a values-aligned buyer. - Created a 3-year timeline to streamline operations, boost revenues, and prepare for a sale.

	Outcome: Established a roadmap aligned with GreenNest's long-term objectives to ensure potential buyers' readiness.
Assess Your Business Valuation	- When it was time, hired a professional valuator to assess GreenNest's financial and operational health. - Compiled detailed financial statements, customer data, and growth projections. **Outcome:** The assessor valued the company 10% higher than Keondra's target and advised her to build a compelling case to justify the company's worth.
Prepare for Sale	- Streamlined inventory management and automated key processes to improve efficiency. - Retained key employees through performance-based incentives. - Settled outstanding debts and improved profit margins. **Outcome:** GreenNest became a well-oiled, attractive prospect for buyers.
Legal Due Diligence	- Conducted a legal audit of all contracts, IP ownership, trademarks, and compliance risks. - Ensured all documentation was organized, current, and transferable. **Outcome:** De-risked the transaction, accelerated buyer due diligence, and minimized legal liabilities.
Prepare for Negotiations	- Defined non-negotiables, including preserving GreenNest's sustainability mission and ensuring employee retention. - Worked with advisors to craft a pitch highlighting growth potential and brand equity. **Outcome:** Approached negotiations confidently, securing favourable terms that protected the company's values.
Identify the Right Buyer	- Targeted buyers with proven commitments to sustainability and market expansion. - Conducted due diligence to evaluate their financial stability and alignment with GreenNest's values and mission. **Outcome:** Partnered with a national retail brand that

	supported eco-friendly businesses and was aligned with GreenNest's ethos.
Contingency Planning	- Kept secondary buyers engaged as a backup in case primary negotiations stalled. - Explored alternative exit options such as mergers or Employee Stock Ownership Plan (ESOP). - She reviewed personal financial and career plans to see if deal terms needed to shift. **Outcome:** Maintained leverage during negotiations and ensured business continuity regardless of deal outcome.
Manage the Transition	- Provided comprehensive documentation, including vendor contracts, operational manuals, and customer insights. - Offered consulting support for six months to guide the new leadership. - Secured retention bonuses for key employees to ensure continuity. **Outcome:** Delivered a seamless handover, maintaining stability for employees and customers.
Protect Your Legacy	- Negotiated clauses to preserve GreenNest's eco-friendly ethos and avoid greenwashing. - Issued a joint public statement with the buyer to reassure customers about the brand's future. **Outcome:** Preserved trust with loyal customers while enhancing the brand's reach.
Maintain Relationships Post-Exit	- Stayed connected with GreenNest's leadership through regular check-ins. - Celebrated milestones with the team and engaged with the community as a brand ambassador. **Outcome:** Fostered goodwill and continued contributing to GreenNest's mission.

Keondra's exit from GreenNest exemplifies a great approach to a successful transition, all thanks to her strategic planning and execution. She exceeded her valuation expectations while ensuring its sustainability mission remained intact. Employees stayed motivated, customers trusted the brand, and GreenNest thrived under its new leadership.

Key Takeaways:

- Plan to take initiatives in advance to optimize the company's worth.
- Align with buyers who respect your mission to protect your legacy and values.
- Ensure a smooth transition to support employees, customers, and future opportunities.

Self-Assessment: Are You Exit-Ready?

Answer the following questions on a scale of 1 (not at all) to 5 (absolutely). Add up your score to see where you stand.

1. Have you assessed the value of your business with the help of a professional?
2. Do you have a clear exit strategy that aligns with your goals and values?
3. Are you aware of the pros and cons of different exit options (e.g., sale, merger, initial public offering - IPO)?
4. Are you prepared to negotiate confidently to get the best deal possible?
5. Have you planned for a smooth transition to minimize disruption for your team and customers?
6. Have you identified and addressed any weaknesses that could impact the value of your business to a buyer?
7. Are you focused on preserving your legacy and ensuring the long-term success of your business?

Score Analysis:

- **30-35**: You're exit-ready - congrats on planning your grand finale.
- **20-29**: You're on the right track, but fine-tune your strategy for maximum impact.
- **Below 20**: Time to get serious about your exit. Start by evaluating your business and exploring your options.

Author's Tip: A strategic exit plan must mirror your goals and values, cover financial and succession aspects, and set you up for future undertakings.

Part 3 - Entrepreneur's Tools

Introduction to Part 3: Entrepreneur's Tools

As an entrepreneur, you're the architect of your business. You are expected to strategically design, construct, and refine your vision until it becomes reality.

However, even visionary leaders need the right tools to bring their ideas to life and navigate the complexities of a business.

In this part, you will discover practical, actionable models and resources to help you manage the challenges of entrepreneurship. Whether you're just starting or scaling your operations, this section provides a robust toolkit tailored to your journey.

This part focuses on three key pillars of entrepreneurial success: foundational frameworks, financial and operational tools, and execution and growth strategies. These tools are not theoretical constructs but actionable resources honed through real-world experience and designed to meet the diverse needs of entrepreneurs across industries.

Section 3.1: Foundational Frameworks lays the groundwork for your entrepreneurial journey. Here, we delve into creating a compelling **Vision, Mission, Values, and Operational Principles** that align your aspirations with strategic intent. We also introduce the **FRAME Blueprint** to develop a strong, scalable business model for long-term success.

Section 3.2: Financial and Operational Tools addresses the lifeblood of any business - its finances and operations. From a comprehensive **Model for Financial Planning** to a pragmatic **Model for Cash Flow Management with Risk and Mitigation**, this part helps you ensure financial stability and resilience.

Section 3.3: Execution and Growth Tools is about scaling your business and maintaining growth. Here, we present a Model for Entrepreneurial Time Management to help you achieve maximum productivity with competing priorities. You will also have a tool that gives you a structured framework that breaks down each sales funnel stage in a clear, organized table format.

Whether navigating your first business idea or refining a growing enterprise, here are some essential entrepreneur's tools as your resource guide for building a robust and prosperous business. This part empowers you to thrive and succeed in the dynamic era of entrepreneurship.

Section 3.1: Foundational Frameworks

3.1.1. The "GUIDE" Blueprint: Craft Your Business's True North

Creating Your Organization's True North requires thoughtful collaboration, strategic alignment and cultural clarity. The **GUIDE Model** simplifies this complex process into simple, actionable steps, ensuring your vision, mission, values, and operational principles resonate at every level of your organization. Here's a detailed breakdown of each stage.

Stage	Actions
G: Gathering Insights - Collect insights from stakeholders and analyze market needs.	- **Engage with Stakeholders**: Gather input from employees, customers, partners, etc. - **Analyze Industry Trends:** Understand market needs and competitive positioning. - **Assess Organizational Strengths:** Identify unique strengths and competencies. - **Document Insights:** Record common themes from feedback.
U: Understanding Purpose - Define a compelling vision and mission statement.	- **Define the Vision Statement:** Articulate a long-term, inspirational goal. - **Define the Mission Statement:** Explain the organization's core purpose. - **Keep Statements Clear and Concise:** Ensure simplicity and memorability. - **Align with Stakeholder Feedback:** Ensure statements resonate with stakeholder insights.
I: Identifying Core Values -	- **Brainstorm Key Values:** Choose values that align with the mission and support long-term goals. - Narrow Down to Core Values: Select 3-5 key values.

Establish core beliefs that shape culture and guide behaviour.	**- Define Each Value Clearly:** Provide descriptions explaining each value in context. **- Ensure Values are Actionable:** Choose values that can be observed and practiced.
D: Defining Operational Principles - Translate values into actionable guidelines for daily operations	**- Identify Principles from Core Values:** Turn each value into specific, actionable principles. **- Align Principles with Mission and Vision:** Ensure each principle supports the organization's purpose. **- Define Practical Examples:** Describe real-life applications. **- Make Principles Flexible and Scalable:** Design for growth and adaptability.
E: Establishing Strategic Alignment - Integrate vision, mission, values, and principles into organizational strategy.	**- Incorporate into Strategic Planning:** Align goals and initiatives with vision, mission, values, and principles. **- Communicate Clearly Across the Organization:** Ensure all team members understand and can articulate the vision and mission. **- Reinforce in Daily Operations:** Integrate principles into processes and evaluations. **- Evaluate and Adjust Periodically:** Regularly review to maintain relevance and alignment.

By following the **GUIDE Model**, organizations can foster clarity, consistency, and alignment, empowering every team member to act purposefully and confidently. When done right, this model transforms abstract ideals into a living framework that drives growth and builds trust internally and externally.

3.1.2. FRAME Blueprint: Building a Business Model That Works

Designing a successful business model is more than developing a revenue stream. It's about determining how your business creates value, makes an impact, and sustains itself long-term. The FRAME Model breaks down this daunting task into simple and actionable steps that assist you in creating a comprehensive and flexible business model. Here's a step-by-step breakdown to guide you through the process.

Stage	Actions
F: Focus on Value - Identify the core value your organization provides.	**- Define Your Value Proposition:** What unique problem are you solving? **- Clarify Customer Needs:** Understand what your customers truly want. **- Assess Differentiators:** Identify what sets your solution apart. **- Validate Value with Customers:** Gather feedback to confirm relevance.
R: Recognize Resources - Identify key resources and capabilities necessary to deliver value.	**- List Essential Resources:** People, technology, intellectual property, etc. **- Map Key Partnerships:** Identify alliances that strengthen your offering. **- Evaluate Operational Capabilities:** What can you do better than anyone else? **- Plan for Scalability:** Ensure resources can grow with demand.
A: Architect the Delivery - Design how you will deliver value to your customers.	**- Define Delivery Channels:** Online, retail, direct sales, etc. **- Optimize Customer Experience:** Ensure smooth and effective delivery. **- Align with Customer Preferences:** Meet customers where they are.

	- **Ensure Efficiency:** Streamline operations to reduce friction and cost.
M: Monetize Strategically - Establish revenue streams and pricing strategies.	- **Identify Revenue Streams:** Direct sales, subscriptions, licensing, etc. - **Set Pricing Models:** Competitive, value-based, or cost-plus. - **Test Revenue Assumptions:** Validate willingness to pay. - **Ensure Sustainability:** Balance profitability with customer value.
E: Evaluate and Evolve - Continuously refine the business model for relevance and resilience.	- **Measure Performance:** Track key metrics tied to value and profitability. - **Gather Ongoing Feedback**: Regularly engage customers and stakeholders. - **Adapt to Market Changes:** Respond to shifts in demand, competition, and technology. - **Innovate Proactively:** Seek new opportunities for growth and impact.

Using the **FRAME Model**, businesses can construct a distinct, consistent, and customer-driven business model. This blueprint ensures all elements of your business are strategically aligned and can adapt to market forces. Implemented well, the FRAME Blueprint transforms ideas into a viable and scalable reality.

Section 3.2: Financial and Operational Tools

3.2.1. The "PROFIT" Model - Master Your Finances

A good financial plan is more than just numbers; it is your road map to growth and success. The PROFIT Model for Financial Planning is aimed at helping entrepreneurs by simplifying the process into manageable steps.

Element	Steps
P: Projections - Develop financial forecasts to create a roadmap.	- **Sales Forecast:** Estimate sales based on market analysis and goals. - **Income Projections:** Create an income statement projecting revenue, Cost of Goods (COGS), gross profit, and net profit over 1-5 years. - **Cash Flow Forecast:** Project monthly inflows and outflows. - **Break-Even Analysis:** Calculate the point where revenue covers expenses.
R: Revenue Streams - Identify and diversify income sources for stability.	- **Primary Revenue Sources:** Identify main revenue-generating products/services. - **Secondary Revenue Sources:** Consider upsells, cross-sells, or new product lines. - **Recurring Revenue:** Explore subscriptions or long-term contracts. - **Revenue Growth Plan:** Strategy to grow revenue streams over time.
O: Operating Costs - Plan and control expenses to maximize profit.	- **Fixed Costs:** List regular expenses (e.g., rent, salaries, insurance). - **Variable Costs:** Forecast costs tied to production or sales (e.g., materials, shipping).

	- Cost-Saving Measures: Identify ways to reduce expenses without sacrificing quality. **- Budgeting:** Set monthly/quarterly budgets.
F: Funding -Determine capital requirements and secure financing.	**- Estimate Funding Needs:** Calculate funds needed for operations and growth. **- Explore Financing Options:** Consider savings, loans, investors, or crowdfunding. **- Develop a Funding Plan:** Outline sources, terms, and repayment expectations. **- Risk Assessment:** Evaluate risks associated with each funding option.
I: Investment Plan - Allocate capital for growth and Return on Investment (ROI).	**- Identify Key Investments:** List major investments (e.g., technology, marketing, hires). **- Set ROI Expectations:** Calculate expected returns to prioritize projects. **- Allocate Capital:** Budget for investments while preserving working capital. **- Risk Mitigation:** Assess risks and create contingency plans.
T: Tracking - Monitor financial performance and make real-time adjustments.	**- Monthly Financial Reports:** Generate income statements, balance sheets, and cash flow reports. **- Compare Actuals vs. Projections:** Analyze variances to improve accuracy. **- Key Performance Indicators (KPI) Monitoring:** Track key financial indicators. **- Quarterly Review:** Update projections and budgets.

By using the **PROFIT Model**, you can establish a good financial base, allowing you to make sound decisions and take advantage of growth opportunities in an ever-changing market.

3.2.2. "FLOWS": Your Cash Flow Compass for Driving Growth

Effective cash flow management is what keeps the business up and running. It brings stability to operations and cushions the blow from unprecedented financial shocks.

The FLOWS Model provides a comprehensive framework for managing cash flow, focusing on key stages from forecasting to managing long-term growth.

The model outlines each stage and integrates actionable steps, risk mitigation strategies, and expected outcomes to assist entrepreneurs and financial managers in maintaining healthy cash flow.

The table below will give you an overview of the FLOWS stages:

Stage	Steps	Risk Mitigation
F: Forecast	**Estimate Revenue and Expenses:** Use historical data and trends to identify this. **Identify Cash Flow Risks:** Factor in demand volatility, delayed payments, or seasonal fluctuations. **Create Best- and Worst-Case Scenarios:** Consider how different scenarios impact the business.	**Establish Contingency Plans:** Plan for worst-case scenarios (e.g., line of credit, delaying non-essential expenses). **Diversify Customer Base:** Don't rely on a few clients for revenue.
L: Limit	**Prioritize Essential Expenses:** Focus on costs critical to operations. **Limit Non-Essential Spending:** Avoid discretionary expenses during uncertain periods. **Establish Spending Policies:** Set guidelines and approval processes for additional expenses.	**Implement Cost-Cutting Measures:** Renegotiate vendor contracts or cut overhead. **Set Up Emergency Funds:** Allocate funds to cover unexpected costs.

O: Optimise	**Accelerate Accounts Receivable:** Offer early payment discounts or late fees. **Negotiate Accounts Payable:** Extend terms or use installment plans. **Optimize Inventory Levels:** Adjust inventory based on demand forecasts.	**Implement Cash Buffer Policies:** Maintain a minimum cash balance. **Revisit Payment Terms Regularly:** Adjust terms with clients and suppliers as needed.
W: Watch	**Conduct Regular Cash Flow Reviews:** Compare actual cash flow to projections. **Identify Trends and Variances:** Spot and investigate variances. **Set Cash Flow Alerts:** Use minimum cash level alerts to prompt actions if levels fall.	**Create Real-Time Dashboards:** Use software to track cash flow instantly. **Engage in Stress Testing:** Simulate adverse scenarios to test resilience.
S: Sustain	**Establish Cash Reserves:** Allocate income to an emergency fund. **Plan for Slow Periods:** Prepare strategies for lower sales periods. **Focus on Customer Retention:** Create loyalty programs for steady cash flow.	**Use Credit as Backup:** Maintain access to a line of credit but avoid regular reliance. **Review Long-Term Financial Strategy:** Ensure the cash flow model supports growth without excessive risk.

This structured overview provides a step-by-step process for proactive cash flow management, ensuring you are prepared for challenges and positioned for long-term success.

Section 3.3: Execution and Growth Tools

3.3.1. The "PRODUCTIVE" Model: Managing Your Time Better

Time is an entrepreneur's most valuable resource, especially for those tackling the challenges of building a business from the ground up. Managing multiple tasks, making vital decisions, and spearheading sustainable growth requires more than just putting in longer hours; it requires working smarter.

The PRODUCTIVE Model is a compilation of tools for managing time designed specifically for entrepreneurs. The model addresses prioritization, planning, and delegation, which allows founders to overcome typical pitfalls like distraction, burnout, and inefficiency. Every model component focuses on connecting day-to-day activity to long-term business goals so entrepreneurs can diligently handle their responsibilities without feeling overwhelmed.

From categorizing tasks using the Eisenhower Matrix to identifying peak productivity windows and establishing firm boundaries, the PRODUCTIVE Model breaks down time management into actionable, easy-to-implement steps. Using this approach, entrepreneurs can cultivate greater focus, make purposeful progress, and reclaim valuable time for innovation and growth.

This table outlines each letter of the PRODUCTIVE acronym with associated action steps and tools to make time management more practical and efficient.

Category & Description	Action Steps	Explanation of Tools
P - Prioritization: Identify the most important tasks to achieve business objectives and eliminate, delegate or	1. List all tasks for the day or week. 2. Categorize them using the Eisenhower Matrix (Urgent/Important).	**Eisenhower Matrix:** A matrix that helps categorize tasks by urgency and importance to identify high-priority items.

outsource low-priority tasks.	3. Focus on high-value tasks.	**Task List:** A simple list for organizing daily, weekly, or project tasks.
R - Review and Adjustment: Regularly review progress and adjust your time management approach based on outcomes and bottlenecks.	1. Conduct a weekly review of completed vs. planned tasks. 2. Identify inefficiencies and plan improvements.	**Reflection Journal:** A personal journal to reflect on wins, challenges, and lessons. **Analytics Tools:** Creates reports or dashboards showing time usage patterns.
O - Overcommitment Avoidance: Learn to say "no" to tasks that don't align with your core business objectives.	1. Assess whether the request aligns with business goals. 2. Politely decline tasks that add unnecessary workload.	**Boundary-Setting Scripts:** Pre-written polite ways to decline or reschedule requests that don't serve your goals (e.g., "I'd love to help, but I can't commit right now.").
D - Daily Planning: Create a structured daily schedule with buffer times for unexpected interruptions.	1. Plan your day the night before. 2. Allocate time for meetings, focus work, and breaks. 3. Use the 80/20 rule to focus on activities driving 80% of results.	**Calendar Apps:** Tools like Google Calendar and Outlook that help schedule and set reminders across devices. **Paper Planner:** A physical notebook for writing schedules and to-do lists.

U - Utilize Time Blocking: Assign fixed times in your schedule for specific tasks or categories (e.g., client calls, strategy, breaks).	1. Divide your calendar into chunks for key tasks. 2. Avoid over-scheduling; leave buffer time. 3. Review weekly to adjust blocks based on priorities.	**Digital Calendar:** Online calendars that visually organize commitments and tasks to avoid scheduling conflicts.
C - Create Task Batches: Group similar tasks to complete them in dedicated time blocks, minimizing context-switching.	1. Identify recurring tasks (e.g., social media updates, emails). 2. Schedule specific time blocks for grouped activities.	**Time Block:** Allocate specific time slots for grouped tasks, making focus time more efficient.
T - Track Energy Levels: Align your most challenging work with high-energy periods of the day.	1. Identify and effectively utilize peak productivity hours (e.g., morning vs. afternoon). 2. Schedule difficult tasks for those times.	**Pomodoro Timer:** helps you to use the Pomodoro Technique. It breaks work into focused intervals, typically 25 minutes, followed by short breaks to improve concentration and productivity. **Energy Journal:** A log used to track energy levels

		throughout the day to optimize scheduling.
I - Improve Delegation: Assign tasks that others can do to save you time for high-impact work.	1. Identify tasks that don't require your direct input. 2. Delegate clearly with timelines and expectations. 3. Regularly follow up, but avoid micromanagement.	**Project Management Tools:** Platforms that help entrepreneurs assign tasks, track progress, and ensure accountability (examples: Asana, Trello).
V - Veto Distractions: Eliminate distractions that consume time and reduce focus.	1. Turn off notifications during focus periods. 2. Use website blockers for distracting sites (e.g., social media). 3. Set dedicated times for emails.	**Focus Mode Tools:** Apps that block distracting websites and track online activity (examples: RescueTime, Freedom) to improve productivity.
E - Establish Goals: Set SMART (Specific, Measurable, Achievable, Relevant, Time-bound) goals to guide time allocation.	1. Break down yearly goals into quarterly, monthly, and weekly goals. 2. Assign deadlines for each.	**Goal Planning Template:** This is very useful in documenting and monitoring the progress of SMART goals. These goals are breaking down long-term objectives into manageable tasks with clear deadlines.

When you implement consistently, this model transforms time from a constraint into a strategic asset, enabling you to achieve your goals without sacrificing your well-being. In a world where every minute counts, mastering time means mastering success.

3.3.2. The "CREATE" Model: Building a Sales Funnel

Introducing the **CREATE Model for Building a Sales Funnel**: This structured framework outlines each sales funnel stage in a clear, organized table format. It provides a detailed breakdown of the core stages - Capture, Reach, Engage, Action, Transition, and Expand - along with actionable steps at each phase to effectively guide prospects from initial interest to conversion and beyond. By following this model, entrepreneurs and sales professionals can ensure a seamless, value-driven journey that fosters engagement, builds trust and drives consistent results.

Stage	Steps
C: Capture -Attract attention and generate leads.	- **Develop Targeted Content:** Use blog posts, social media, videos, and advertisements to speak to your ideal customer's interests and pain points. - **Optimize for Search and Social:** Leverage SEO and social media strategies. - **Use Lead Magnets:** Provide downloadable content in exchange for contact information.
R: Reach -Nurture initial interest and build relationships.	- **Welcome Sequence:** Send a series of emails introducing your brand, values, and solutions. - **Educate with Valuable Content:** Share resources that address the lead's needs and pain points. - **Segment Leads:** Group leads by interests, behaviour, or demographics.
E: Engage -Build trust and demonstrate the value of your offerings.	- **Provide Case Studies and Testimonials:** To build credibility, share reviews and success stories. - **Offer Product Demos:** Use webinars, live demos, or free trials to let leads experience your product. - **Address Pain Points Directly:** Tailor content to common objections.

A: Action -Drive leads to take action, such as purchasing or scheduling.	**- Present a Compelling Offer:** Provide a discount or limited-time bonus. **- Use Strong Calls To Action (CTA):** Ensure clear, direct, and strategically placed CTAs. **- Personalized Follow-Up:** Follow up with personalized messages or calls for high-value leads.
T: Transition - Facilitate smooth onboarding for new customers.	**- Welcome New Customers:** Send a message that sets expectations and makes customers feel valued. **- Provide Onboarding Resources:** Share tutorials, FAQs, or support contacts. **- Encourage Initial Engagement:** Guide customers through early steps to experience value.
E: Expand -Build loyalty and encourage referrals to grow the customer base.	**- Collect Feedback and Act:** Seek feedback and act on it. **- Offer Loyalty Rewards:** Reward repeat purchases or referrals. **- Engage With High-Quality Content:** Keep building customers with unique promotions and information.

This model enables businesses to reach prospects where they are, address their needs proactively, and deliver seamless, impactful experiences. By being focused on building trust and nurturing relationships at every stage, your business ensures that your sales funnel becomes a powerful engine for sustainable success. Whether you are refining an existing funnel or starting from scratch, the **CREATE Model** will assist you in getting consistent, quantifiable outcomes while developing meaningful connections with your clients.

Bonus Content

Business Plan Framework

This **comprehensive** business plan **framework** provides a step-by-step walkthrough of every section, including helpful tips and things to avoid. It has illustrative examples to make the key objectives clear and helps solidify your understanding. Every section states its purpose and highlights examples to assist you in clearly and effectively communicating your business's strategy, market position, and operational plan. This framework empowers entrepreneurs to build a well-structured plan that resonates with investors, stakeholders, and internal teams. The following guide explains each section of the business plan, and you will also find detailed examples to inspire your business plan.

1. Executive Summary

Purpose:

This is the first section, but it's written last as it summarizes the entire plan! It gives readers a high-level overview and helps them decide whether to keep reading. This section must be concise and engaging.

What to Include:

- Business Concept: A brief description of what your business does.
- Mission Statement: The "why" behind your business - your purpose.
- Vision Statement: Your big-picture goals and where you're heading.
- Financial Goal: Revenue targets, funding requirements, and timeline.

Tips for Success:

- Keep it short (1-2 pages max).
- Write it in simple and plain language - skip technical jargon.
- Make it exciting - show your passion and ambition.

Common Mistakes:

- Making it too long or too vague.
- Forgetting to mention key financial goals.

Example:

- Business Concept: "Novalution Edge is a tech start-up offering custom software development and a SaaS platform designed to improve business efficiency."
- Mission: "Transforming tech chaos into clarity with cutting-edge solutions."
- Vision: "To be the global leader in user-centric software solutions."
- Financial Goal: "Reach $1.5M in annual revenue by Year 2 and $3M by Year 3."

2. Mission, Vision, and Value Proposition

Purpose:

This section explains your business, where you are headed, and what makes you different. It sets the tone for the rest of the plan.

What to Include:

- Mission: Your company's purpose and why it matters.
- Vision: Your long-term goals and what success looks like.
- Value Proposition: A short, powerful statement about your business's unique benefits.

Tips for Success:

- Keep your mission clear and inspiring.
- Make your vision future-focused - paint a picture of success.
- Your value proposition should focus on the customer and how you solve their pain points.

Example:

- Mission: "To simplify tech complexities and deliver high-performing software solutions."

- Vision: "To be the preferred tech partner for startups and SMEs by 2030."
- Value Proposition: "We combine custom software expertise with SaaS reliability to meet unique business needs."

3. Industry Analysis

Purpose:

Show that you understand the industry you're entering. Investors want to know if you've researched the market and understand the trends, challenges, and opportunities.

What to Include:

- Market Overview: Facts and data about the industry (size, growth, trends).
- Target Market: Who are your ideal customers? What are their demographics, behaviours, and needs?
- Competitive Landscape: Identify key competitors and explain how you're different (your competitive advantage).

Tips for Success:

- Use recent market research and credible sources.
- Clearly explain your niche and how you'll stand out.
- Include charts or graphs to make the data more digestible.

Common Mistakes:

- Being vague about your target market.
- Failing to acknowledge competitors.

Example:

- Market Overview: "The SaaS market is projected to grow to $374B by 2026."
- Target Market: "Small businesses and startups in industries like finance and healthcare."

- Competitive Landscape: "Competitors include Company A (fast delivery) and Company B (low-cost services). We differentiate by focusing on reliability and customization."

4. Strategy

Purpose:

Your strategy outlines your game plan - how you will achieve your goals.

What to Include:

- Goals: Key milestones (e.g., number of customers, revenue targets).
- Business Model: How you will make money (subscription fees, product sales, etc.).
- Strategic Priorities: The actions you'll take to hit your goals.
- Unique Selling Proposition (USP): What makes your business stand out?

Tips for Success:

- Be specific - set measurable goals (e.g., "gain 200 customers by Year 2").
- Explain your pricing model clearly.
- Align your strategy with your target market's needs.

Example:

- Goals: "Acquire 200 SaaS customers and complete 50 software projects by Year 2."
- Business Model: "Subscription-based pricing for SaaS; project-based fees for custom software."
- Strategic Priorities: "Enhance customer onboarding, automate processes, and invest in customer support."
- USP: "Combining custom software expertise with SaaS reliability."

5. Marketing and Sales

Purpose:

Explain how you'll attract customers and close sales.

What to Include:

- Marketing Plan: Your strategies for reaching your target audience (e.g., social media, content marketing).
- Sales Strategy: Your approach to converting leads into customers (e.g., free trials, demos).
- Customer Acquisition Cost (CAC): How much you'll spend to gain one customer.

Tips for Success:

- Focus on your ideal customer - where do they spend their time?
- Show how your marketing plan aligns with your goals.
- Include metrics to back up your approach (like conversion rates).

Example:

- Marketing Plan: "We'll use blogs, webinars, and social ads to drive traffic."
- Sales Strategy: "Offer free trials and use case studies to build trust."
- CAC: "Projected CAC is $300, with a customer lifetime value (CLV) of $6K per SaaS customer."

6. Operations

Purpose:

Describe how your business will run on a day-to-day basis.

What to Include:

- Operational Plan: Key tasks and workflows for product development, delivery, and support (e.g., inventory checks, sales calling, client servicing, etc.).
- Technology and Tools: The software and systems you'll use (e.g., website host, CRM tools).

- Quality Assurance: How you'll ensure high standards (e.g., uptime monitoring).

Tips for Success:

- Focus on efficiency - show how you'll save time and money.
- Highlight your use of automation and tools.
- Be clear about responsibilities - who's doing what?

Example:

- Operational Plan: "Daily tasks include SaaS monitoring, client onboarding, service fulfillment, and product updates."
- Technology: "Using AWS (Amazon Web Services) for hosting and HelpScout for customer support."
- Quality Assurance: "Weekly code reviews and continuous system monitoring."

7. Team

Purpose:

Highlight your team's expertise and structure.

What to Include:

- Leadership Team: Key people and their roles.
- Organizational Structure: How your team is organized.
- Talent Plan: Your hiring and growth plans.

Tips for Success:

- Include relevant experience - show why your team is capable.
- Use bios and resumes as appendices if needed.

Example:

- Leadership Team: "CEO Kai Granger (10 years in tech entrepreneurship), CTO Saleem Balser (software implementation expert), COO Sarah Lee (over 7 years experience in operations)."

- Organizational Structure: "Flat hierarchy encouraging collaboration."
- Talent Plan: "Hire three developers and one customer success specialist in the next 12 months."

8. Financial Numbers

Purpose:

Show your expected revenue, expenses, and funding needs.

What to Include:

- Revenue Projections: How much money do you expect to make?
- Expenses: Your fixed and variable costs.
- Profit and Loss: Your projected net income.
- Funding Needs: How much capital do you need to grow?

Example:

- Revenue Projections: "Year 1: $500K, Year 2: $1.5M, Year 3: $3M."
- Expenses:

"Fixed costs (year 1): $600K annually for salaries and tools. There is a 50% increase in fixed cost in years 2 and 3."

"Variable costs: 15% of revenue for marketing. An additional 20% variable cost for custom software."

- Net Profit Margin: "Expected to reach 25% by Year 3."
- Funding Needs: "Seeking $1M in seed funding."

9. Appendices

Purpose:

Include supporting documents and data.

What to Include:

- **Market Research:** Reports showing demand.
- **Financial Tables:** Detailed revenue and expense breakdowns.
- **Resumes:** Team bios and key achievements.

Tips for Success:

- Only include relevant materials - don't overwhelm readers.

Investor Pitch Playbook: Nailing Your First Impression

While pitching to investors, first impressions are everything. When you step into a room to pitch your business idea, you're not just presenting facts and figures - you're sharing your vision, your story, and the potential for what could be. Investors want more than a solid business plan; they want to believe in *you*. This playbook is designed to help you build that belief.

Crafting a winning investor pitch requires more than just knowing what to say - it's about structuring your narrative in a way that resonates, persuades, and inspires action. Whether you pitch to angel investors, venture capitalists, or partners, every slide in your deck has a purpose. Each section sets out the essential components of a successful pitch, complete with crucial tips and presentation hacks to help you impress.

This guide will guide you on how to:

- Draw your audience in with a compelling introduction
- Present your market opportunity like a seasoned strategist
- Highlight your competitive advantage and traction to build credibility
- Leave a lasting impression by closing with confidence and clarity

Every brilliant business idea deserves an equally great pitch. This playbook will equip you with the tools to present your business with clarity, confidence, and impact. After all, an investor presentation isn't just about raising funds - it's about building partnerships that drive your growth.

Okay, let's get started and create a pitch that turns heads and opens doors!

1. Hook Them from the Start (Title Slide)

What to Include:

- Company Name and Logo
- Tagline that embodies your mission
- Your Name and Title

Tip:

Set the stage with attractive and appropriate graphics (because picture says a 1000 words) and crisp branding - first impressions count!

2. Bring the Problem to Life (Problem Statement)

What to Include:

- A brief statement of the problem you're solving
- Data points or a compelling anecdote illustrating the pain point

Tip:

Be authentic - make your audience feel the problem. Avoid jargon and keep it human.

3. Show the Hero in Action (Solution)

What to Include:

- Clear explanation of your product/service
- A "wow" moment: how you solve the problem in a way others can't

Tip:

Use an analogy or a visual demo to make the solution unforgettable.

4. Paint the Big Picture (Market Opportunity)

What to Include:

- Total Addressable Market (TAM), Serviceable Addressable Market (SAM), and your niche
- Data or trends validating growth potential

Tip:

Keep it visual - simple bar graphs or infographics can transform dry numbers into powerful insights.

5. **Explain the Money Machine (Business Model)**

What to Include:

- Revenue streams and pricing strategy
- Customer acquisition approach

Tip:

Imagine you're answering, "How do you make money in your sleep?" Keep it simple and focus on profitability

6. **Flaunt Your Wins (Traction)**

What to Include:

- Key metrics like sales growth, downloads, partnerships
- Timelines or graphs to highlight momentum

Tip:

Milestones matter. Highlight your "Aha!" moments - proof your idea works!

7. Outshine the Competition (Competitive Advantage)

What to Include:

- Side-by-side comparison with competitors
- Your unique strengths (e.g., proprietary tech, expertise, partnerships)

Tip:

Use a competitor matrix or positioning grid to visually demonstrate your edge.

8. Chart the Financial Path (Financial Projections)

What to Include:

- 3 - 5 years of revenue, expenses, profit margins
- Break-even point and expected ROI

Tip:

Be confident but honest. Your projections should balance ambition with realism.

9. Steering Growth and Innovation (The Dream Team)

What to Include:

- Key team members, their roles, and expertise
- Advisors or key partners to add credibility

Tip:

People invest in people. Use photos and punchy bios to create a personal connection.

10. Make the Ask (Funding Request)

What to Include:

- The funding amount you need
- How you'll allocate funds (e.g., R&D, marketing, operations)

Tip:

Break it down. Pie charts or tables make your budget plans crystal clear.

11. Leave Them Inspired (Closing Slide)

What to Include:

- Reinforce your vision and potential impact
- Contact details and a call-to-action (e.g., "Let's connect!")

Tip:

End with energy - your last slide should leave your audience excited to partner with you.

Startup Failures: Key Insights and Lessons Learned

Introduction:

Understanding why startups fail is just as valuable as analyzing why they succeed. This section examines 25 startups that ultimately shut down despite initial promise and funding. Their stories offer critical lessons for entrepreneurs on what pitfalls to avoid.

Studied the following 25 failed startups:

▪ Pets.com	▪ Solyndra	▪ Secret
▪ Webvan	▪ MoviePass	▪ Vine
▪ Quibi	▪ Quirky	▪ Yik Yak
▪ Theranos	▪ Shyp	▪ Fab.com
▪ Beepi	▪ Color Labs	▪ Bodega
▪ Juicero	▪ Brandless	▪ Zirtual
▪ Better Place	▪ Anki	▪ Sidecar
▪ Homejoy	▪ Rethink Robotics	▪ Homepolish
		▪ Stayzilla

Takeaways from the Analysis:

This analysis highlights some of the most common mistakes that led to these failures. Whether it was misreading market demand, over-engineering a product, scaling too quickly, or failing to manage cash flow, these examples reveal the importance of staying agile, customer-focused, and financially disciplined. Below is a visual depiction of the analysis of why the companies failed. For detailed case studies and additional resources, visit - www.wildboldandambitious.com

The following Pie Chart is a visual representation of the reasons the start-ups failed:

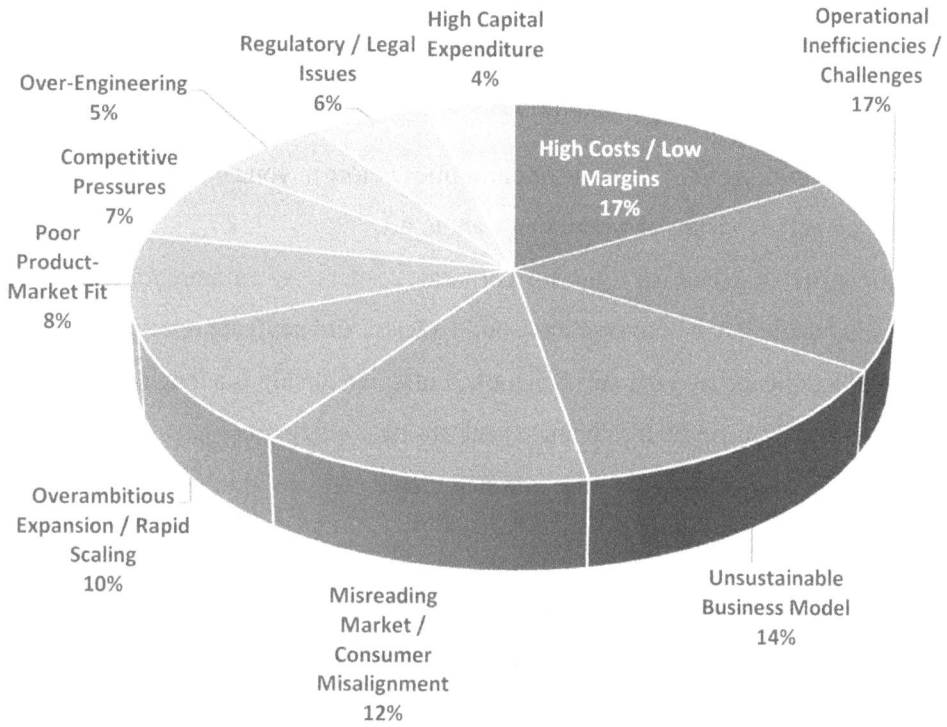

Failure Reason

Key Takeaways for New Entrepreneurs

If you're stepping into the world of entrepreneurship, this playbook is your blueprint. The "Wild, Bold, and Ambitious" walks you through the traits you need, the journey you'll take, and the tools to keep you moving forward. Here's what you, as a new entrepreneur, should walk away with:

1. Success Starts With Who You Are, Not What You Do

Your personal traits will be your greatest assets - or your biggest liabilities. The most successful entrepreneurs share a common DNA:

- Visionary Thinking helps you see opportunities before anyone else does. Develop a clear, compelling vision of where you want to go.

- Emotional Intelligence isn't just for corporate leaders. As an entrepreneur, it will help you handle tough conversations, build a team, and navigate rejection.

- Grit and Resilience are your survival tools. Entrepreneurship is a long game - expect setbacks and train yourself to bounce back stronger every time.

- Confidence and Self-Belief are non-negotiable. If you don't believe in your business, no one else will.

Insight for You: Start by developing your mindset. Cultivate these traits intentionally. You can have the best product or service in the world, but if you lack resilience and belief, you won't last.

2. Agility Is Your Superpower

Markets shift, customer needs evolve, and obstacles show up when you least expect them. Your ability to **adjust and pivot** will define your longevity.

- Adaptability and Flexibility: Don't fall in love with your first idea. Be ready to tweak, change, and reinvent.

- Risk-Taking: Smart risks separate the doers from the dreamers. Don't let fear freeze you - use data and instinct to make bold moves.

- Resourcefulness: Most new businesses start with limited funds and manpower. Learn to make the most out of what you have.

Insight for You: Being nimble isn't a luxury - it's a necessity. Build flexibility into your business plan and stay close to your customers to understand what they need as they evolve.

3. You Can't Build Alone: Relationships Are Currency

The **people** you know - and how you treat them - are just as important as your product.

- Networking and Relationship-Building are critical for finding partners, investors, mentors, and customers.
- Customer-Centric Mindset: Your business exists to solve problems for others. Deeply understand your customers and put them at the center of every decision.

Insight for You: Prioritize relationships from day one. Attend events, ask for introductions, and serve your customers like they're your business partners - because they are.

4. Execution Beats Ideas

A great idea is worth **nothing** without solid execution.

- Strong Work Ethic: Be prepared to do the unglamorous work - long hours, tedious tasks, and constant problem-solving.
- Financial Acumen: Learn how money moves in and out of your business. Understand your cash flow, margins, and runway.
- Operational Excellence: Smooth daily operations differentiate between a thriving business and one that dies from chaos.

Insight for You: Fall in love with the grind. Great businesses are built on a thousand small, consistent actions, not one genius move.

5. Build With the End in Mind

Even if you're starting, think about where you're heading. Whether scaling, selling, or passing the business on, **long-term thinking** will help you make better decisions today.

- Long-Term Perspective: Avoid short-term wins that undermine your long-term vision.

- Exit Planning: Knowing how and when you want to exit helps you align strategy, operations, and investor relations.

Insight for You: Clarify your endgame early. Do you want freedom? A legacy? A buyout? Your goals will shape how you grow.

6. Follow an Established Framework, Don't Reinvent the Wheel

You don't need to figure it all out from scratch. Use **structured tools and frameworks** to guide your growth:

- The GUIDE Blueprint helps clarify your vision and align your team.
- The FRAME Blueprint ensures you build a business model that works.
- The PROFIT Model and FLOWS Framework keep your finances healthy.
- The PRODUCTIVE Model maximizes your time and focus.
- The "CREATE" Model assists in building a Sales Funnel and drives sales growth with an efficient, scalable funnel.

Insight for You: Follow a map. There are tested models in this book that save you from unnecessary trial and error. Lean on them.

7. Social Impact and Responsibility Matter

Today's customers and investors care about more than just profits.

- Doing Well by Doing Good: Businesses that positively impact society often outperform those that don't.
- Social Responsibility isn't optional anymore - it's expected.

Insight for You: Build your values into your business from day one. People support companies that stand for something bigger than themselves.

8. Learn From Failure - Especially Other People's

The book's **analysis of failed startups** reveals patterns:

- Poor cash flow management
- Lack of product-market fit

- Weak leadership and team dynamics
- Failure to adapt
- Burnout and loss of passion

Insight for You: Study why others fail and proactively address those issues in your business. You don't have to make every mistake yourself to learn from it.

Bottom Line

This book is more than a guide; it's a **field manual for entrepreneurship**. It shows you what it takes to succeed from the inside out: developing your traits, navigating the journey, leveraging practical tools, and learning from real-world examples.

If you absorb and apply these lessons:

- You'll build a business rooted in strong personal traits
- You'll be prepared for challenges and growth
- You'll have tools to scale and sustain
- You'll create something that lasts

Now, it's up to you to leap.

Disclaimer

This book is intended to provide practical guidance and insights for new entrepreneurs. While every effort has been made to ensure the relevance of the information, the content is based on personal experiences, observations, and research. It may not apply to every situation or individual.

The strategies, tools, and examples presented in this book are meant to inspire and inform; however, they should not be considered a substitute for professional advice. Readers are encouraged to consult with qualified legal, financial, or business advisors to address specific concerns or decisions related to their unique circumstances.

The author and publisher disclaim any liability for outcomes resulting from using the information in this book. Business success is influenced by many factors, including but not limited to market conditions, individual effort, and external variables beyond the scope of this book.

Entrepreneurship is inherently a journey of learning and adaptation. Readers are encouraged to use this book as a guide, but ultimately, the responsibility for decision-making rests with the individual entrepreneur.

By reading this book, you acknowledge and accept that the author and publisher are not liable for any actions or decisions based on its content.

www.ingramcontent.com/pod-product-compliance
Lightning Source LLC
Chambersburg PA
CBHW062031210326
41519CB00061B/7436